35.96

JOSEF + ANNI ALBERS
Designs for Living

JOSEF + ANNI ALBERS
Designs for Living

MERRELL
LONDON · NEW YORK | Cooper-Hewitt, National Design Museum

First published 2004 by Merrell Publishers Limited

Head office
42 Southwark Street
London SE1 1UN

New York office
49 West 24th Street
New York, NY 10010

www.merrellpublishers.com

in association with

Cooper-Hewitt, National Design Museum
Smithsonian Institution
2 East 91st Street
New York, NY 10128

www.cooperhewitt.org

Published on the occasion of the exhibition
Josef and Anni Albers: Designs for Living
Cooper-Hewitt, National Design Museum, Smithsonian Institution
October 1, 2004 – February 27, 2005
.

British Library Cataloguing-in-Publication Data:
Weber, Nicholas Fox, 1947–
    Josef and Anni Albers : designs for living
    1.Albers, Josef, 1888–1976 2.Albers, Anni 3.Designers – United States
    4.Designers – Germany 5.Interior decoration – United States 6.Interior
    decoration – Germany 7.Furniture design – United States 8.Furniture
    design – Germany 9.Textile design – United States 10.Textile design –
    Germany
    I.Title II.Filler, Martin
    745.4′0922

ISBN 1 85894 264 0

Produced by Merrell Publishers
Designed by Geoffrey Winston
Copy-edited by Matthew Taylor
Indexed by Christine Shuttleworth
Printed and bound in China

Jacket front: Josef Albers, *Upward*, *c*. 1926 (detail of pl. 22)
Jacket back: Josef and Anni Albers. Photograph by Henri Cartier-Bresson

The extracts from Josef Albers's letters to Franz Perdekamp on pp. 152–53
appear courtesy of the heirs of Franz Perdekamp. They were translated
by Ingrid Eumann. The extract from *Wohnoekonomie* was translated by
David Blocher.

CONTENTS

6   **Foreword**
Paul Warwick Thompson

8   **Designs for Living**
Nicholas Fox Weber

32   **A Marriage of True Minds**
The Designs of Josef and Anni Albers
Martin Filler

56   **The Works of Josef and Anni Albers**

150   **Excerpts from the Writings
of Josef and Anni Albers**

157   **Further Reading**

158   **Index**

FOREWORD

The Smithsonian's Cooper-Hewitt, National Design Museum is proud to present this exhibition of iconic and rarely seen objects of domestic life by two leading twentieth-century artists and designers, Josef and Anni Albers. For the first time this exhibition will bring together a little-known facet of Josef's career—his furniture, graphic art, and tabletop objects—with Anni's designs and textiles, some of which have never been exhibited before. This extraordinary collection of designs for everyday living affirms the intrinsic role design played in their life, influencing equally their choice of clothes to wear, food to eat, and material to use in their furniture or textiles. Ironically, Josef and Anni never collaborated on a specific project, yet they lived collaboratively, perpetually guided by a single aesthetic philosophy that sustained them throughout their life: to remain faithful to materials and purpose, while striving for an elegance derived from simplicity and a reassertion of the bare essentials.

As the only American museum dedicated exclusively to historical and contemporary design, Cooper-Hewitt, National Design Museum is the ideal stage for exploring the work of Anni and Josef Albers. Through their essays Nicholas Fox Weber, Executive Director of The Josef and Anni Albers Foundation and guest curator of the exhibition, and Martin Filler explore how design not only impacted on the Alberses' life but also steered it in a direction that became influential for future generations of artists. Excerpts from the Alberses' personal letters, essays, and unpublished notes, also included in this book, reveal their commitment to shaping the physical world around them and, during their lifetime, provided another way of disseminating their beliefs and ideas.

No one can speak or write more assuredly, enthusiastically, or engrossingly about Josef's and Anni's life than Nicholas Fox Weber. This presentation and publication would not have been possible without the collaboration and very generous support of the Albers Foundation. We are equally grateful to Maharam for their early and very timely support for the show.

The lenders have all been extremely generous with their objects, and we are especially grateful to Mrs. Esther English and The Art Institute of Chicago for making it possible to exhibit together, for the first time, furniture designed by Josef for the Moellenhoff apartment in Berlin. At the Art Institute we would like to thank Dr. James Wood (former Director), Ghenete Zelleke (Curator of European Decorative Arts), Barbara Hall (Conservator), Mary Solt (Registrar), and Matthew Cooke (Assistant Director, Imaging). At the Museum of Modern Art, New York, we are indebted to Glenn D. Lowry (Director), Terence Riley (Chief Curator in the Department of Architecture and Design), Christian Larsen (Senior Cataloguer in the Department of Architecture and Design), Lynda Zycherman (Conservator), Karl Buchberg (Senior Conservator), and Mikki Carpenter (former Director of Imaging Services) for graciously coordinating this significant loan of works at a very busy time.

For their generosity, cooperation, and support throughout the research and execution of this exhibition and book, we are grateful to the following: at the Busch-Reisinger Museum, the Harvard University Art Museums: Thomas W. Lentz (Director), Marjorie Cohn (Carl A. Weyerhaeuser Curator of Prints), Peter Nisbet (Curator), Craigen Bowen (Conservator and Deputy Director of Conservation), Lisa Lee (Curatorial Assistant), and Dorothy Davila (Visual Resources); at the Albers Foundation: Brenda Danilowitz (Chief Curator), who masterfully handled many details, Sandrine Vallée-Potelle, Stephane Potelle, Oliver Barker, John Miele, and Molly Wheeler; at the Bauhaus-Archiv in Berlin: Dr. Peter Hahn (former Director),

Dr. Annemarie Jaeggi (current Director), Christian Wolsdorff (Senior Curator), and Sabine Hartmann; at Die Neue Sammlung in Munich: Dr. Florian Hufnagl (Director), Dr. Josef Strasser (Curator), and Tim Bechtold (Department of Conservation).

In addition, Nicholas Fox Weber would like to acknowledge Rupert Deese, John and Andrea Weil, and Arne Glimcher, as well as Jerl Surratt for his seminal role in helping to originate this exhibition, Eames Demetrios for his support and guidance, and Leslie and Clodagh Waddington for their perpetual insights into the Alberses' way of seeing. He is grateful to Geoffrey Winston for the attention and understanding brought to the design of this book; to Hugh Merrell, Julian Honer, Sam Wythe, and all at Merrell Publishers for their perpetually high standards and attention to the quality of the publication; and, again, to Oliver Barker at the Albers Foundation for his artistic intelligence and personal grace while attending to such a myriad of details. He also would like to thank his wife, Katharine Weber, and daughters, Lucy Swift Weber and Charlotte Fox Weber, for their specific and helpful memories of life in the Alberses' household and of time spent with Anni; and, as always, John Eastman and Charles Kingsley, his fellow trustees of The Josef and Anni Albers Foundation, for their unflagging support.

Toshiko Mori, the exhibition designer, maintained beautifully the delicate balance of quality versus quantity and, in so doing, adhered to the Alberses' own principles regarding the spare interior. From the office of Toshiko Mori Architect we would like to thank Jolie Kerns and Wendy Cronk.

And, finally, the Cooper-Hewitt staff did an outstanding job of managing the organization of the exhibition. The process was superbly supervised by Exhibitions Curator and Head of Textiles Matilda McQuaid, whose input and guidance have been essential throughout the process. I would also like to thank the following individuals: Barbara Bloemink (Curatorial Director), Susan Brown (Curatorial Assistant), Lucy Commoner (Conservator), Jocelyn Groom (Head of Exhibitions), Chul R. Kim (Museum Editor), Steven Langehough (Registrar), Sandra Sardjono (Assistant Conservator), Lindsay Stamm Shapiro (former Exhibitions Coordinator), and Scott Wilhelme (former Head of Installations).

Paul Warwick Thompson
Director
Cooper-Hewitt, National Design Museum
Smithsonian Institution

DESIGNS FOR LIVING

Nicholas Fox Weber

Shortly after Josef and Anni Albers moved into one of Walter Gropius's flat-roofed, planar Masters' Houses at the Dessau Bauhaus, Josef, who was the first Bauhaus student appointed to the faculty, told the somewhat apprehensive Anni, his bride of three years, thirteen years his junior and a student in the weaving workshop, that Ludwig Mies van der Rohe and Lily Reich, Mies's mistress, would be coming for dinner. Anni wanted to do everything right. The house was meticulously organized. Josef's sandblasted glass constructions—all pure abstractions, some of them lean and minimal exercises in black and white, others jazzy syncopations of vibrant color—were lined up in a row on the living room wall. The arrangement was noticeably strident, a brave declaration of hard work and serious purpose, and a deliberate eschewal of prettiness. Marcel Breuer's Wassily chairs—not the production numbers known worldwide today, but the first prototypes, made three years earlier, of this early foray into the use of tubular steel formerly consigned to bicycle handlebars—were positioned against the walls in a pose more sculptural than friendly, so that their users looked at space rather than at one another, a statement about strength and solitude in the world, in complete opposition to the look of coziness that was the norm in Germany at that time. Josef's own furniture designs, all spare and ornament-free, provided seating and surfaces with the straightforward, candid voice essential to these young *Bauhäusler*. Even the one potted plant looked restrained and understated. Anni wanted the details of the dinner to reflect the same degree of care and forethought, and to show respect for the great architect, older than her husband, who would soon be the third Bauhaus director, and hence her and Josef's boss.

Anni's mother had given her a butter curler. In the household in which Anni had grown up—a lavish and capacious apartment in a five-story nineteenth-century building on Meinekestrasse, just off the Kurfürstendamm in Berlin—family members never entered the kitchen, which was strictly reserved for staff. But when dinner was laid out on the heavy, carved Biedermeier table in the ornament-laden dining room, butter balls were part of the landscape, and Anni knew how they were made. Preparing for dinner that evening in Dessau, she carefully used the clever metal implement to scrape off paper-thin sheets of butter and form them into graceful, delicate forms resembling flower blossoms. It was the sort of process and manipulation of material she prized. Like weaving, the making of butter balls required the careful stretching and pulling of a supple substance with the correct tool, and achieved a transformation.

Mies and his notoriously imperious female companion arrived. They had not even removed their coats or uttered a word of greeting before Reich looked at the table and exclaimed, "Butter balls! Here at the Bauhaus! At the Bauhaus I should think you'd just have a good solid block of butter."

It was a sting Anni Albers remembered word for word sixty years later, and a story she told with relish as she sat in her raised ranch house in the Connecticut suburb of Orange and looked back on a lifetime devoted to making art a part of every aspect of human existence. As a person, she was inclined to describe herself as victim. She often recalled slights or insults, perhaps to accentuate the true victories of her life, her surmounting of formidable obstacles. But the significance of Lily Reich's remark was not just its nastiness. The incident revolving around the form of butter on the dining room table exemplified the way that every detail of how we live, every aesthetic choice, affects the quality of daily human experience.

The difference between a block of butter and a butter ball is aesthetic: a hard form as opposed to a lacy, open one, a "this is what you get" event as opposed to a more slowly seductive moment. It also

(previous page)
Josef and Anni, c. 1935.

The Alberses' living room in their Masters' House at the Dessau Bauhaus, with furniture and glass constructions by Josef, as well as two of the original Wassily chairs (among the first ever made) by their friend and colleague Marcel Breuer.

has sociological importance: the distinction between a sight that reflected the old world of upper-class Berlin, with its fancy and intricately nuanced way of life, and the new world embraced by the pioneering art school in Dessau that concerned itself with design for the masses.

"Art is everywhere!" Anni and Josef used to exclaim euphorically of the Mexican villages they discovered after the Nazis forced the closing of Mies's Berlin Bauhaus in 1933 and they had emigrated to America. Within a year of their exile from their native country, they had begun a series of wonderful journeys from Black Mountain College in North Carolina, their base for sixteen years. Josef had been summoned to Black Mountain because the new and experimental school was looking for a dynamic figure who could make art the focal point of the curriculum. Margaret Lewisohn, a friend at New York's Cosmopolitan Club of Ethel

Dreier, the mother of one of the founders of Black Mountain, had heard of the search, and had asked her young cousin Edward Warburg if he had any ideas. Warburg, who was working gratis at the Museum of Modern Art, New York, raised the question with Philip Johnson—another unpaid MoMA employee, just in the process of starting up its department of architecture and design, and not yet a certified architect. Together Warburg and Johnson had instantly settled on Albers's name, since both of these young American men had visited the Dessau Bauhaus a couple of years earlier.

Johnson invited Anni and Josef, in an event that also revolved around Lily Reich. In June 1933, Johnson had run into Anni on a street in Berlin, and she had asked him for tea at her and Josef's new flat in the Charlottenburg area. In this radically austere space with white linoleum floors, Johnson looked at

View from the living room into the area with the guest bed at 808 Birchwood Drive in Orange, Connecticut. The Alberses were particularly pleased when a five-year-old visiting the house pointed out that the off-center arrangement of the air-conditioning vent in the ceiling was exactly the same as in one of Josef's paintings. They considered this sort of "seeing" much more impressive than the work of art historians.

some of Anni's textile samples and suggested that Lily Reich had given herself credit for the very same pieces. He somehow wanted to right a wrong. It was that summer that Eddie Warburg had walked down the corridor linking his and Johnson's offices at MoMA and mused about who had the necessary charisma and wisdom to teach art at Black Mountain. With that in mind, Johnson asked Josef and Anni if they would be interested in coming to America. Knowing that the Nazis' disdain for Modernism suggested a dark future for them in Germany, and that Anni's Jewish background was likely to pose problems in their lives, they were enthusiastic. Shortly after he returned to New York, Johnson spoke with the people at Black Mountain and sent a telegram inviting the Alberses. They had no idea where North Carolina was, and somehow thought it might be in the Philippines, but after doing some research and hearing that it was a friendly place with a beautiful climate, they sent back word that they would like to come. They warned, however, that Josef spoke no English.

Johnson and Warburg instructed the Alberses by return telegram to come anyway. Unknown to the former *Bauhäusler*, Warburg footed the bill for their steamship tickets. The day after their ship docked in New York in late November 1933, the Alberses were taken within a block of what is now the Cooper-Hewitt, National Design Museum to Warburg's parents' house (today the Jewish Museum) to see the collection of Rembrandt prints and Italian Renaissance fakes. They instantly thrilled to New York, its lights and vitality, and to the way its museums, unlike the sleepy institutions in Berlin, were perpetually crowded with eager viewers. At Black Mountain the Ionic columns of the all white Neo-classical Robert E. Lee Hall offered a major surprise to Anni, who could not understand how paper notices could be thumb-tacked into marble, but who learned quickly enough that in

America columns could be made of wood. Josef set about teaching and soon overcame his language problems to inform adoring students, "I want to make open the eyes," which he quickly shortened into the words that would define his purpose in life forever after: his goal was "to open eyes."

His own eyes were perpetually being opened further, especially when, within a year of arriving at Black Mountain, he and Anni, in Ted and Bobbie Dreier's Model A Ford, made their way southwest and across the Texas border to those Mexican villages, where they were stunned by the way that the descendants of the great civilizations of Maya and Zapotec lived richer lives than they had ever seen before. The Alberses marveled at the designs of serapes and ponchos, the beauty of the ancient pottery, the charm of the hand-painted earthenware being produced in small villages, the architecture of even the simplest hut. This was the guiding principle: aesthetics are not confined to a single area of life, certainly not to painting or weaving alone (these being the Alberses' specialties), but count immeasurably in all choices in life and, moreover, affect the way we breathe, the way we feel at every waking moment, our sense that all is right in the world or that something is painfully wrong.

In the early 1970s, when Josef was at the peak of his fame and success, I had occasion to revisit with him one of the souvenirs of those junkets south of the border. It was a telling encounter. Josef, at age eighty-four, was in good form. He had recently been the first living artist to be honored with a solo retrospective at the Metropolitan Museum in New York. The greatest living photographers had been coming to call and take his picture—Cartier-Bresson, Karsh, Penn, Snowdon, and Newman had all recently snapped the red-faced artist, with his shock of smooth white hair and look of all-consuming intensity. (Part of the routine of these occasions was

(overleaf)
Anni and Josef at the Dessau Bauhaus. Photograph by Marianne Brandt

for the Alberses to take the photographer, as well as the visiting dignitaries and museum people and interviewers who came to call, to a new steak restaurant, the Plank House, on the commercial strip near to their house. What delighted them above all in this establishment on the Boston Post Road were the laminated tables. Josef was amazed by the shiny plastic coating, which was so easy to sponge clean. And they were equally impressed by the salad bar, a new invention of the time, its range of choices under a transparent dome seeming a sort of modern marvel.) There had been television documentaries, a lot of newspaper coverage, and so on; moreover, for the first time in his life he had begun to make enough money not to have to worry about paying the bills.

We were sitting at the kitchen table one winter afternoon. The table was white Formica, from Sears Roebuck; the chairs, also from Sears, were tubular steel, with the seats and backs covered in plain white plastic. The walls were entirely blank, with nothing at all on them except for the thermostat, which was a bronze-colored eyesore. The kitchen cabinets— standard stock—and appliances were almost all there was to look at, the most distinguished objects in the laboratory-like setting being an original Chemex coffee maker (given to Josef by its inventor, Dr. Schlumblum) and the Salton yogurt maker that Anni used on a daily basis to give Josef one of his

favorite foods, not yet generally available.

Suddenly Josef began to fly into a rage while he was eating his apple strudel and sipping coffee. The red of his face brightened and deepened as he explained that in the *New York Times* that day there was an interview with Robert Motherwell. Josef disliked Motherwell's work, just as he despised most exponents of Abstract Expressionism (he would say that Jackson Pollock "paints with his tail"). Josef ranted, "They ask Motherwell what he achieves in his art, and he says 'eternity.' Not even Michelangelo, not even Leonardo, not even Piero, would say that! Who thinks he achieves eternity? Motherwell!"

The octogenarian jumped to his feet. In his L.L. Bean tattersall shirt and khaki pants, he resembled the sort of robust New Englander who worked in traditional hardware stores with creaky wooden floors. He rushed over purposefully to the kitchen counter and picked up a small object, with which he returned to the table. He then put down the hand-painted Mexican bird that had been cupped in his hand. It was a simple pottery form, the body ample and curvaceous, the head delicate, the surface covered with bright, feathery, abstract patterns painted in brilliant blues, reds, greens, and pinks.

"You see this bird. It comes from a little village in Mexico. There are thousands like it, everywhere, in every village. We will never know who the artist

Anni in the kitchen at 8 North Forest Circle, New Haven, Connecticut, 1958.
Photograph by Lee Boltin

The Alberses' kitchen at 808 Birchwood Drive, Orange, Connecticut, where they moved in 1970.

was. But this bird captures more of eternity than Motherwell with his nonsense."

Art that is modest in intention, that does not refer to its maker but rather evokes his subject, that is competent and unpretentious, that serves its purpose, and that brings simple pleasure into everyday life: here was the Albersian ideal.

The kitchen was always a good place to be with Josef and Anni. Nuances of food preparation and presentation counted heavily in their lives. This was one of the many arenas in which design, process, sensory experience, and the essential elements of human existence all came together for them. Proportion, balance, clear thinking, and organization are all vital in the kitchen, both for practical effectiveness and emotional satisfaction, and the Alberses were closely attuned to the details. They often made the links between the activities of cooking and eating and the making and consuming of so-called high art. When people would ask Josef how he painted his *Homages to the Square*, his routine answer was, "I paint the way I spread butter on pumpernickel." "Spread" became "Schpread" with his Westphalian accent, and he would say "Pumpernickel" slowly, delighting in its origin as "Pain pour Nicole," Nicole having been a horse, the only creature the French deemed able to tolerate the black, Westphalian-style bread they disdained. Albers liked to emphasize that earthy simplicity; he was proud of his working-class origins, of that part of his personality that connected more with coarse multi-fibered bread the color of tar than with a baguette. His father had been a house painter, carpenter, electrician, general contractor, and fix-it: someone who had taught the young Josef how to do almost everything, and to do it well.

Craft, professionalism, and working the right way were what counted—as opposed to the self-revelations and what Albers considered the ultimate narcissism

of German Expressionism, most especially that practiced by Max Beckmann. Albers would show people the backs of his *Homages to the Square*, where he had neatly written out the name of each color, complete with the manufacturer of the paint, and would refer to this information as "the recipe." He would tell students to "schmier" their paint— delighting in the robust inelegance of that word, which sounds so much like what it is, and which applies as much to chicken fat, in particular the German specialty *Griebenschmaltz*, one of the most unrefined foods imaginable.

The implication, of course, was that to paint a good painting and cook a good dish are much the same. You take well-chosen ingredients, assemble them in correct quantities, and put them together systematically. Nothing fancy, please. Don't make grandiose claims. And understand that a simple domestic activity—the following of a recipe, the spreading of butter on a piece of honest black bread, redolent of the earth, full of character and nourishment—is noble.

That interaction between everyday living and artistic creativity, between the practical and the spiritual, permeated Josef's and Anni's life. An extremely earnest art critic from New York once came to interview Josef about the *Homages to the Square*, in the late 1960s, after fame and fortune had struck because of these paintings (which Albers used to call, with yet another food service analogy, his "platters to serve color"). The critic looked at the septuagenarian Albers and began his dead-serious inquiry. "Mr. Albers, we have noticed that, after years of painting your *Homages* in sizes ranging from 16 by 16 inches to 40 by 40 inches, in 1964 you expanded to the scale of 48 by 48. Was this, Mr. Albers, your response to the vast scale of American Expressionism, to the oversized canvases preferred by the forces who had taken over the art scene? Or did it have to do

with your experience of coming to the United States as a European and encountering the vast landscape of the prairie and the Rockies? Or, perhaps, Mr. Albers, was this a reaction to the beginning of the space program, to this era when satellites were heading into the larger universe as never before?" Josef looked the young critic in the eye, fixed his gaze, and furrowed his brow. "Young man, that was the year we got a larger station wagon."

He wasn't entirely joking. These are the things that count in life; our everyday details affect how we work on every front, even the most artistic and spiritual. Cars were a big thing: Josef and Anni both loved to drive, especially after they moved to Connecticut in 1950, and, as with butter balls and blocks of butter, cars were as symbolic as they were practical. When Anni was new at the Weimar Bauhaus, having bravely given up her elegant childhood to live simply in a rented room where she was allowed a bath only once a week, having defied her bourgeois upbringing by trying to make her way in the pioneering art school, she had been totally humiliated one day when two of her uncles showed up to visit in their spanking new Hispano-Suiza. She made them park where no one could see this symbol of the affluence she had spurned. Years later, in Connecticut, she and Josef had been thrilled when they could afford a new Chevrolet, especially one with room for those larger paintings. And then they indulged in what, for them, with their generally puritanical and modest taste, was the greatest material luxury of their lives: a Mercedes 240. Josef loved the name of the color: "English racing green," with its suggestion that a hue could represent the dash and charms of the racetrack. Moreover, they both liked the sense of security offered by that weighty car. And for Josef, who had been poor as a child, who had struggled for nearly half a century to have enough money to live, who had always had to teach and write in order to fund his existence as a painter, a Mercedes was, admittedly, a symbol of success, his one public acknowledgment that, in old age, he had made it.

Naum Gabo, another daring modern artist and Albers's contemporary, had the exact same car; the year, model, and color were identical. Albers knew this because he and Gabo shared warehouse space in New Haven. Albers, however, had no time for Gabo's

*Anni and Josef at home at 8 North Forest Circle, New Haven, c. 1965.
They had moved into the house in 1950.* Photograph by John Hill

(overleaf)
*Josef and Anni at home at 8 North Forest Circle, New Haven. They
preferred to display work by Josef's students rather than their own designs.*
Photograph by Henri Cartier-Bresson

Constructivist sculpture; Gabo may well have felt the
same way about Albers's rows of *Homages to the Square*,
which were in the same storage vault. The only subject
the two could discuss without acrimony, on the
occasions when their visits to the warehouse coincided,
was their cars. At the loading dock the two dark
green Mercedes sedans would often be parked side by
side. And two of the leading artists of the twentieth
century, too old to want to disagree about art, would
be standing there politely asking one another about
the optimum moment to put in antifreeze or the
maintenance of the saddle-colored leather seats.

From the making of high art to car references and
cooking recipes, from the ethereal and even religious
spheres to the everyday: these transitions, these
links, were natural and utterly essential to Anni's
and Josef's life. Josef liked to tell people that his
father had taught him that, when you paint a door,
you start at the center and work your way out so
as to catch the drips and keep from getting your
cuffs dirty. This, therefore, was how he painted the
Homages: always, without exception, making the
center square first, putting the paint straight from
the tube on the white background, as he did with
each and every color. The results were astounding,
full of an inexplicable glow, similar to stained glass
and cathedral spaces, rich in their offerings, but the
origins were simple and practical.

When Josef was painting those *Homages*, and Anni
was making her extraordinary woven wall hangings
and designing textiles for drapery and upholstery
material and other areas of everyday life, they
looked at every aspect of their daily existence with
the same sense of careful measurement, the same
process of evaluation, as they used in choosing paint
color and thread. Their appearance mattered greatly
to them; there was a noticeable resemblance between
them, and each was groomed with great care but
always with an abiding simplicity. Josef was always

clean-shaven, and used the term "those bearded
ones" pejoratively; he hated the look of deliberate
bohemianism. If the Bauhaus was like the Gothic
cathedral, a place where craftspeople from every
realm worked together in the service of God, the
Alberses believed that artists were people in service
of a religion, who should in their appearance embody
order and diligence. Anni was obsessed with her hair,
which had been unusually thick (in contrast to Josef's
fine strands) when she was young. What she mainly
wanted from it was a look of tidiness as well as the
best possible form. They both dressed, for the most
part, in neutral colors—Anni more often than not
in a white blouse and beige or khaki skirt (pants
late in life), Josef in a gray or tan shirt and trousers
of similar hue. The idea was that nothing should cry
out for attention, or suggest a fad or trend; rather,
the details of clothing should embody quiet good
taste. That choice was brave and unusual, especially
once fashion designers prevailed in selling logos and
convincing the public that it was good to advertise
their wares with insignias that signify high price and
approved status—none of which had any influence on
the Alberses' choices.

Anni cared not about brand names but about
the nature of the weave, the cut of a jacket, the
appropriateness of the form to the purpose, and the
practicality. She derided the emphasis on "all natural"
or "hand-woven," which became buzz words of an
ecology-conscious society. Rather, she loved uttering
the term "drip-dry"—which, with her lilting Berlin
cadences, became "dahrip-dahrie," sounding as if
little beads of water were gently falling downward.
If "drip-dry" meant polyester, hence synthetic, that
was perfectly fine. One of the last true thrills of her
life was the discovery of "ultra-suede," a material
that, regardless of its name, was also man-made and
synthetic. She was delighted with the way she could
travel overseas wearing it and get off the plane

without a wrinkle, and she thought the physical lightness and visual simplicity of the soft substance, as well as the way it was clearly a product of careful research in a laboratory rather than of the natural world, were all impressive.

What all of this reveals is a constant, unified aesthetic. Isaiah Berlin, in his essay on Tolstoy entitled *The Hedgehog and the Fox*, characterizes hedgehogs as those "who relate everything to a single, central vision, one system, less or more coherent or articulate, in terms of which they understand, think and feel—a single, universal, organizing principle in terms of which alone all that they are and say has significance." By contrast, foxes, the other type of human being, are "those who pursue many ends, often unrelated and contradictory, … related by no moral or aesthetic principle." The Alberses were hedgehogs; more remarkably, they were the same hedgehog.

Anni's bedroom in the Masters' House at the Dessau Bauhaus, c. 1928. The figurine on the shelf is a reproduction from a Berlin museum that Josef gave her on her twenty-third birthday, June 12, 1922.

In what they said, what they wore, what they drove, where they lived—and, most importantly in their personal hierarchies, the art they both produced, varied as it was—there was complete consistency. The intention was faithfulness to purpose as well as to the components, a respect for effective process, and a soothing, beneficent appearance. Everything was done with an eye for balance and rhythmic grace. Judgment was vital. Choices had to be made, and one had to choose what was effective and, in the true rather than the frivolous sense of the word, elegant.

The values that Josef and Anni both cherished, that prevailed in the house where they ended their days in Connecticut as they had in that Masters' House in Dessau, were of a piece for more than half a century. The furniture that Josef designed at the Bauhaus was in the idiom of the time, closely resembling designs by Marcel Breuer and Eric

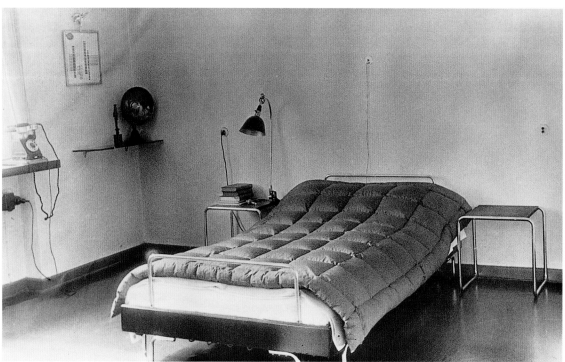

Dieckmann, and other Bauhaus furniture makers, but it was simpler, leaner, and more minimal than anyone else's. Just as the *Homages to the Square* would, nearly a quarter of a century later, reduce painting to a new level of simplicity, so Josef's chairs and tables were a getting down to bare essentials, bold and spare like the virtually monosyllabic language of King Lear at the very end of Shakespeare's play, when he is grasping at the raw truth and nothing else.

Josef's chairs are also one step more graceful than those of other designers. Indeed, they are a painter's designs, conceived with a particularly sophisticated artistic eye. Josef constructed furniture with the flair of a subtle abstractionist laying out his forms and colors on the canvas. When we see his tables and other pieces from the mid-1920s we think that, yes, they are of the period, but they strike us with aesthetic nuances that their peers lack. Josef's furniture is the bridge between design and art, between a household object and a painting by Klee or Kandinsky. It is boldly drawn, conceived, like his later *Structural Constellations* (a body of work that was realized as engravings on vinylite, prints, and paintings), as drawings in space. The checks and balances and graceful progress into three-dimensionality make this furniture quite sublime. Moreover, Josef plays their wood tones against each other—dark timber against light—with the same eye that later in life created some of his most refined *Homages to the Square*. As a furniture maker, he was drawn by instinct to linear rhythm and angular play, to tonal harmony, to an understanding that everything in the visual world is about context and the relationship of one element to another. When you arrive at Josef's work after seeing Dieckmann's and Breuer's and that of the other leaders, you get, then, both a levity and a richness that distinguish it.

Josef's desk for Fritz Moellenhoff and his armoires for the Moellenhoffs' bedroom anticipate Donald Judd's Minimalism by some thirty years. They are noticeably bold, an enticing blend of simple shapes and complex visual results. These courageous objects mix austerity and luxury to an unprecedented degree. The proportions of each armoire are like a segment of one of Josef's *Homage to the Square* paintings. For the hedgehog who made them always valued the tension that can exist when symmetry and asymmetry function in tandem, when a form moves in one direction two-dimensionally and another three-dimensionally.

Nearly everyone who made furniture at the Bauhaus did stacking tables. All of them were simple and devoid of ornament. But Josef's have a crisper geometry, and a lighter spirit. In comparison, the work of his confrères had leaden feet, while his stand on tiptoes. The framing elements of his stacking tables are as light as can be, and the luminosity of their glass tops, in four contrasting colors, provides the infusion of life. Those tops are like the small and vibrant windows in Le Corbusier's chapel at Ronchamp. The miracle of light passing through a solid material without breaking it becomes analogous to the Annunciation, and the sight is luxurious and celebratory.

Anni, too, transformed into an art form what in other hands was merely design work. She elevated textiles and the status of woven threads, and put the medium on equal footing with oil on canvas and watercolor on paper. Buckminster Fuller, himself such an innovator and such a devotee of design for the larger population, affirmed, "Anni Albers, more than any other weaver, has succeeded in exciting mass realization of the complex structure of fabrics. She has brought the artist's intuitive sculpturing faculties and the age long weaver's arts into historical successful marriage."

She had taken up weaving reluctantly. Anni had wanted to be a painter, a fully fledged artist, just like the men who attended the Bauhaus around her. Then, when circumstances and the unalterable realities of her milieu got in the way, and she was told that the weaving workshop was the only one open for her at Weimar, she succumbed to one truth by transforming another. She redefined the possibilities of the medium and blazed a new trail in the territory into which she had been forced— so that the notion of the realm of textile designers was forever after expanded, and they could now be indisputably deemed to be artists. If weavers of previous generations had replicated the flower patterns and decorative motifs that were prescribed for the form, Anni used her yarns to create "visual resting places" (a term she borrowed from one of her heroes, the writer and philosopher Wilhelm Worringer) that are as calming and diverting as they are infinitely rich and complex. Others of the Bauhaus weavers were working with unprecedented clarity as well, and, like Josef, she was initially of a place and time, but, also like Josef, she gave the breadth of art to her interlaced threads. The colors are truly sublime, the looping of threads magical. A great and responsive eye is present in every knot and every choice of fiber.

Paul Klee, Anni's artistic hero and the form master of the weaving workshop, had counseled students to "take a line for a walk." "I let thread do what it could," Anni once reminisced to me. "Kandinsky said, 'There is always an *and*,'" she recalled on another occasion. This, too, nourished her work immeasurably: there are always further links and knots, additional surprises and visual footnotes.

A pioneer of abstract art when it was still a radical concept, in the 1920s Anni made wall hangings of incomparable power and flair and visual excitement. The direct effects and echoes of her daring search have been far-reaching. Abstract wall hangings have come to flourish as an art form. It has become

completely acceptable for thread to be its own voice. At the same time as she put miracles of playfulness and intelligence on the walls, she did so in fabrics to hang as room dividers, in upholstery materials, in draperies, and in rugs that brought diversion and vitality to the floor. What she cherished in one arena she prized everywhere.

At the Bauhaus, Josef worked in practically every workshop except for weaving: he tried his hand at glass, metalwork, woodworking, and wallpaper. He taught courses on the fundamentals of art. Anni was confined, at least officially, to the realm of textiles. But all of these categories and divisions were only superficial. Their concerns spread in every direction, from the design of stationery to the making of abstract art, from the placement of objects on the kitchen table to the layout of forms in a large visual composition. These wonderfully determined hedgehogs sought balance, honesty, refinement, clarity, and effectiveness at every waking moment. Waking, indeed, because the visions of sleep—the life of their dreams—was, like the natural world, full of elements beyond their control. While the Surrealists focused on such aspects of existence, those mysteries of the unconscious, the Alberses, in all that they created and selected, sought the opposite. And while they loved aspects of the natural world, they also saw it as full of hazard and difficulty, where domination and even killing often ruled. Life itself was rugged, with inflation and politics, prejudice, war, internecine strife, greed, even evil, often ascendant. But in art, and design, in what we make and use and wear, in the forms of bookshelves and the weave of scarves, the rugs underfoot or the tables next to our beds, we can have some respite, some calm. So Josef and Anni aspired to a consciousness of a luminous, Zen-like beauty, a spirited inventiveness, the seriousness of playfulness, in each and every choice and creative act.

Anni's bedroom at 808 Birchwood Drive. She still had the same reproduction from a Berlin museum at her bedside as she had done sixty-five years earlier. The bedspread was a drip-dry synthetic material from Sears Roebuck, and the encyclopedia on the bookshelf was one that she bought for one dollar per volume at the local supermarket.

A different view of Anni's bedroom. She was pleased to have found the storage units at an office furniture store. The painting is Josef's Equal but Unequal, *from 1939.*

Josef wrote:

To design is

To plan and organize

To order, to relate

And to control.

In short, it embraces

All means opposing

Disorder and accident.

Therefore it signifies

A human need

And qualifies man's

Thinking and doing.

Not just the substance but also the careful spacing of those phrases, the moments for catching one's breath as well as the launching of new thoughts, was deliberate. Anni used to say that a fifteenth-century Korean pot could makes her knees feel different and cause her to breathe in a new way; this was the power of art, of gracefulness, of articulation coupled with artistry. And both the Alberses felt that life could be profoundly enhanced not just by what they actively designed—the tea glasses where one handle was horizontal so that it was easy for the server to pass, the other vertical so that the recipient could easily take it; where ebony and glass and metal provided a rich and harmonious combination of textures, shiny, rough, opaque, transparent—but also by what they chose. If the radio knobs in the Mercedes were the right size for human fingers, and turned at the correct tempo, then they were wonderful things; if the proportions were wrong, or they came off in your hands, then they were a form of evil.

Speaking at a design conference in the 1950s, Josef also declared (the layout of the phrases is from the typescript of his talk):

So I am looking forward

To a new philosophy

Addressed to all designers

—in industry—in craft—in art—

and showing anew

that esthetics are ethics,

that ethics are source and measure

of esthetics.

It was the gospel, their mutual credo, the linchpin of their approach to life, and the intention of their work.

Design was, and had to be, everywhere. On May 12, 1955, when Josef was traveling to Germany to teach with Max Bill in Ulm, Anni sent him a letter, addressing him as "Juvel." She neglected to mention that it was their thirtieth wedding anniversary—they never openly acknowledged such events. But in her own quiet way she was referring to the occasion by providing more than the usual details of everyday existence. She wrote, "When you left, took taxi to Abercrombie and Fitch and bought myself a really good coat, reversible, tweed and rain-coat inside-outside, think you will approve, expensive too, 73.77. In other stores saw nothing that looked quite right. So now I have a good one too. Hope yours works out well." (For their fiftieth wedding anniversary—May 12, 1975—I asked if I could organize a celebration. Anni was adamant that I should never mention the date to Josef. Afterwards, she told me that they had driven to Litchfield, Connecticut, in the Mercedes that day. There was beautiful spring weather and, as always, they enjoyed the meticulously painted white clapboard houses in that perfect colonial town, where

Josef's bedroom at 808 Birchwood Drive. He designed the desk when he was at Black Mountain College. He never hung anything whatsoever on the walls, which he preferred to keep blank, and generally had a volume of nineteenth-century German Romantic poetry at his bedside.

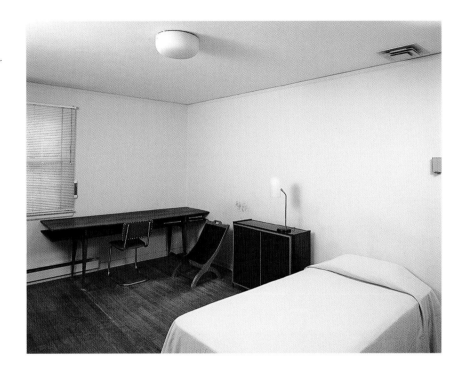

The living room at 808 Birchwood Drive. For the lighting fixture over the stairs, in order to find anything simple enough, Anni went to a store on the Boston Post Road that sold furnishings for patios and porches, and purchased a fixture that had this plain cylinder at the core once she had removed a number of metallic flowers. King-lui Wu often pointed out that the potted palm made it impossible for people to see each other when having a conversation between the two sofas, but the Alberses refused to move it.

they had a good lunch. "We never shouted at each other, all day long, and when we got home, I saw that Juppi had circled the date on his calendar, so he certainly knew," Anni told me. It was their last wedding anniversary before his death.)

How strongly appearances counted. Later in the 1955 letter she described an encounter with an important art critic at Josef's exhibition at the Sidney Janis Gallery. "At Janis met Stuart Preston, good looking, but we had nothing to say to each other, but liked the way he looks." And then, reporting on life at the home front in Connecticut, she reported, "Here greatest news: that Northrop across the street has planted a tiny pink blooming tree in front on the lawn. Eat pumpernickel and to bed early. Yesterday started painting your closet, all holes fixed … The weather is fine, the house smells of paint. Your closet is glistening." She wrote every couple of days. Nearly two weeks later, she put, for the date of a letter, "83 more days so its May 25, 55" and informed "Juvel," "The tulip tree in full bloom, the Rhododendron full

of buds. The house full of paint smell. Your bedroom and your studio now are beautifully finished. White walls downstairs, polished floors, fresh oilcloth on your shelves downstairs." How conducive they were to work, how energizing, these clean and efficient materials. Then came information on the cost of simonizing the Chevrolet, car repairs being a recurrent theme in the correspondence, along with descriptions of lunches with various people, the simple fare as well as the well-being of various friends always part of the report.

Another letter was dated "June 7, 55 (70 more)" and contained the description, "In our living room I put the sofas now like this: 90 degrees to each other, and the room looks bigger and less long I think. Wonder if you will approve, easy enough to push back again." Later came the information, "Bought myself some light colored and washable cotton slacks for Maine. Of all places it was finely [sic] Sears Roebuck where I found some decent ones, had tried Abercrombie etc. And there too I bought myself a

birthday present, a little gray metal typewriter table on rollers, charming, only 7.50 amazingly enough … think you will like it and seems just right to roll around in my room. At least that's what I think … so love and love from Ankele."

On June 12, her birthday, "Ankele" wrote "Juvel" that she had been studying an old bill for flatware "which gives no. for the specific pieces so that you can tell size, style, etc. from that, I think. If not, I'll draw outlines. 4 more forks, knives, soup spoons, coffee spoons, I think." For in Germany he could add to their stainless steel of streamlined design, a patternless pattern that was lightweight and well proportioned. A week later—"58 more, Sunday, June 19.55"—she proposed, "How about getting for yourself a bayrisches blaues linen jacket? You know the kind you used to have? Maybe even one for me? Size 18, amer."

When he received that letter, Josef underlined the information on Anni's size. (If, indeed, it was an 18, it was because she wanted it vastly outsized; a 10 would have been ample for her slight figure.) Josef got her the jacket … and bought himself one as well. They were like a two-person religious sect, this couple who had been nurtured in such totally different worlds but who came together at the Bauhaus. In every aesthetic choice they were allies. They believed that the accouterments of life embodied intelligence, even wisdom, and imparted fabulous charm in a world where so much else was uncertain, even treacherous. For Anni and Josef, whether they were at home at their kitchen table or divided by an ocean, were joined, wonderfully, by their faith that what was material could also be spiritual, that the tangible and the intangible were in many ways the same.

A MARRIAGE OF TRUE MINDS
The Designs of Josef and Anni Albers

Martin Filler

Among the indisputably great couples who left an indelible mark on mid-twentieth-century American art and design—a select group that included Lee Krasner and Jackson Pollock and Ray and Charles Eames—a unique place was held by Anni and Josef Albers. Unlike the case of Krasner and Pollock, the wife did not deliberately subordinate her talent to her husband's and temporarily abandon her career to promote his. Unlike the Eameses, the Alberses were not co-professionals and direct collaborators, although their work in disparate media, especially at the Bauhaus in the 1920s, ran on closely parallel tracks, with notable cross-influences. And although the Alberses spent the most productive decades of their working lives in the United States, their formative experiences in Weimar Germany and their high standing among the remarkable roster of creative émigrés from Hitler's Europe set them apart from their younger, American-born contemporaries.

Although Josef Albers today is best remembered for his *Homage to the Square* series of paintings and prints, and Anni Albers for her weavings, their activities in a far wider range of pursuits remain much less familiar to the general public. As paragons of the comprehensive attitude toward art and design advanced by the Bauhaus, the Alberses—Josef in stained glass, furniture, and graphic design, and Anni in jewelry and printmaking—made no arbitrary hierarchical distinctions among the media they pursued. This no doubt was easier for Josef than for Anni, for he was primarily identified as a high artist, while she chafed at the lesser classification of craftsperson. They arrived at their ultimate *métiers* circuitously and, in the case of Anni Albers, haphazardly. But their excursions in a variety of disciplines only enriched their sense of art and design as being integrally interwoven into the fabric of a modern way of life, and not merely an optional adjunct to it.

The first works by either of the Alberses to attract attention at the Bauhaus were Josef's early essays in stained glass. On completing the school's compulsory *Vorkurs*, or preliminary course, in 1920, Albers entered the stained glass workshop, one of the specialized crafts studios to which students were assigned after their introductory indoctrination. The tangent of Albers's work in glass over the following decade can also be seen as emblematic of the general evolution of the Bauhaus aesthetic from Expressionism to Minimalism over the same period. (Albers would take exception to any of his works being linked with Expressionism, for he deplored what he saw as the movement's subjectivity and revelation of personal emotions—the antithesis of his artistic philosophy.)

Two of Albers's stained-glass panels of 1921 suggest the influence of Paul Klee, one of the three initial teachers of the *Vorkurs* (along with Johannes Itten and Wassily Kandinsky). One untitled work (pl. 18) is made from pieces of discarded colored glass that Albers scavenged from the Weimar town dump because he could not afford conventional artists' materials. (Anni Albers's first recollection of meeting her future husband, when she arrived at the Bauhaus in 1922, was of him prepared for one of those retrieval expeditions, a rucksack on his back and a sledgehammer in his hand.)

This rich assemblage incorporates the curved bottoms of three bottles in green, red, and yellow, along with a colorful spectrum of shards in blues, greens, yellows, and orange, and is held together with metal wire, screen, and gridwork, all within a rough metal frame. The dark background, glowing color, and semi-abstract references to nature evoke Klee's fantasy pictures of the late 1910s and early 1920s, suggesting gardens or landscapes beneath the celestial orbs of the sun or moon.

More rationalized is a second glass panel of 1921, *Grid Picture* (fig. 1; pl. 17). This almost square

(previous page)
Josef and Anni at Dessau, c. 1925.

FIG. 1   JOSEF ALBERS   *Grid Picture*, 1921   (detail of pl. 17)

framework of small glass sample pieces contained within the modules of a sheet of fence latticework relates to a number of Klee compositions from the mid-1910s onward, beginning with the watercolors he made at Kairouan in Tunisia, where he was inspired by the town's cubic architecture. (The flat-roofed, whitewashed buildings of North Africa had an equally strong effect on the architecture of Le Corbusier, just as the similar vernacular structures of the Spanish town of Horta de Ebro did on Picasso's breakthrough Analytic Cubist paintings of 1909.) In Klee's gridded pictures a checkerboard effect of multicolored squares defines the picture plane, a device he was to return to, most often in non-representational form, recurrently over the next two decades.

By about 1924, when he made *Park* (pl. 19), Albers had reached a far more refined level of abstraction. Here the leaded surrounds of the glass squares and rectangles—themselves much purer in texture and tone than his found materials—are meticulously fabricated, in contrast to the panels of three years earlier. Though Albers has relinquished the immediacy of his earlier approach, he nevertheless retains the aura of spirituality that the Expressionists found in colored glass.[1] In this rectangular panel a row of eight vertical milk-glass segments imply a church tower and nave, and this ecclesiastical reference is underscored by four pink panes below it, joined by leading in the shape of a Latin cross. The surrounding "park"—a flattened landscape of monochromatic fields of blues, greens, and golds, and a checkerboard parterre of blue and white—is easily legible in the formal terms (if not the typical bilateral symmetry) of Baroque garden design.

In the following year Albers moved away from the medieval leaded-glass technique altogether and began working in sandblasted glass, which gave his panels a flatter profile and removed the necessity for metal framing to hold separate colors apart. The differences between the two methods were immediate and enormous. Suddenly he could marshal discrete squares and bands of color without external framing, and the outcome made for an entirely different, and more modern, kind of surface.

Josef Albers's *Goldrosa* of *c.* 1926 (pl. 21), a Minimalist composition of sandblasted pink flashed glass with a surface application of black paint, typifies the restrained qualities of his new process. Its pronounced warp-and-weft structure, one cannot help thinking, may well reflect the works that his young wife, whom he had married the previous year, had been producing during her apprenticeship in the Bauhaus weaving workshop. Or did the influence flow in the opposite direction?

There is no question that Anni Albers's horizontally banded textiles of 1925 and 1926 relate closely to Josef Albers's glass panels of those same years, and they offer the clearest proof of the interchange of ideas between the two. But no matter which of them was the source of the motif, both artists showed their ability to develop it in a wholly convincing and completely personal manner. For example, Josef's special interest in color as a central determinant of formal perception—the underlying project of his *Homage to the Square* series—is given an early expression in the identical compositions of *Goldrosa* and *Upward*, also of *c.* 1926 (pl. 22). The latter, in deep blue sandblasted flashed glass with a surface application of black paint, differs from the dusty pink *Goldrosa* only in its predominant color, but Albers shows what a huge difference that "only" can cover, for even side by side the two pieces read as entirely different compositions.

By about 1929 Albers's journey from Expressionism to Minimalism in glass was complete, a transition confirmed by *Skyscrapers on Transparent Yellow* (fig. 2; pl. 20), an almost perfectly square panel of yellow sandblasted glass with black paint. (A black-

FIG. 2 JOSEF ALBERS *Skyscrapers on Transparent Yellow, c.* 1929 (detail of pl. 20)

and-white variant of the identical composition can be seen in a photograph of Anni's bedroom in Dessau from *c.* 1928; see p. 24.) Here black-painted horizontal bands are used to suggest the stories of three slender, flat-topped towers—schematic approximations of International Style skyscrapers that had been proposed in visionary drawings but not yet executed. (The first to be completed would be George Howe and William Lescaze's Philadelphia Savings Fund Society building of 1932, the narrow south elevation of which bears a close resemblance to Albers's imaginary structure.) Equally spaced layers of thin horizontal lines, left unpainted, suggest an urban context around the towers in the most economical manner imaginable. This reductivist masterpiece brings to mind Ludwig Mies van der Rohe's assertion that he wanted his Minimalist, glass-walled architecture to be *beinahe Nichts*—"almost nothing"—although here Albers, like Mies, proves how much can be achieved with very little indeed.

The future Anni Albers, born Annelise Fleischmann, came from a family of rich Berlin *Taufjuden* (Jews who had been formally baptized but not truly converted to Christianity). At the already marriageable age of twenty-two she rebelled against her conventional background and went south to Weimar to study art at the most radical school in Germany. She, like the other young women who enrolled there, was dismayed to discover that the spirit of equality espoused in Walter Gropius's idealistic Bauhaus Manifesto of 1919 had, by the time of her arrival three years later, been supplanted by a much more traditional assignment of gender roles. Gropius, astonished by the large numbers of women who sought admission, backtracked on his original idea that all the school's disciplines should be open to all students and declared, "We are fundamentally opposed to the education of women as architects."

After completing the mandatory *Vorkurs*, Anni, like all the other *Bauhäusler*, was compelled to choose a specialized workshop for the next phase of her education, but none of the choices open to her was very appealing. As she recalled in an oral history interview years later:

> I wasn't at all interested in those workshops really. Because the metal workshop I felt was painful to the hands. The woodworking workshop was so terribly hard, lifting lumber and so on. The wall painting I couldn't stand. I'd be standing on a ladder and getting dirty every day. In the distance I saw my [future] husband in the glass workshop, in the stained glass workshop. And I thought that was rather intriguing. The material and the men working and him in the distance there, you see. And I was told that there wasn't a chance to get into that workshop because there were so very few chances to execute a stained-glass window. And there was one man that was already there; that was all. So the only thing that was open to me was the weaving workshop …
>
> I didn't like the idea at all in the beginning because I thought weaving is sissy, just these threads. And there was a very inefficient lady, old lady, sort of the needlework kind of type, who taught it. And I wasn't a bit interested. But the only way to stay at that place was to join that workshop.[2]

There cannot have been a much more fortuitous "choice" of *métier* in the annals of modern art than this. What may on the surface seem like Anni Fleischmann's princess-like disdain for the toil and trouble of the more strenuous Bauhaus studios was probably a wariness born of her frail physical constitution, weakened as she was since childhood by various ailments. But her reluctant acceptance of the one workshop that allowed her to remain in proximity to the interesting Josef Albers was a most beneficent accident of fate. The glorious and prolific output of Anni Albers over the next five decades, until she gave up weaving in 1970, defines the single most impressive œuvre of a twentieth-century fabric artist.

Yes, Albers's longevity did play a role in her ultimate ability to reposition her ranking among her Bauhaus contemporaries, especially *vis-à-vis* her principal rival there, the weaver Gunta Sharon-Stölzl. Survivors can rewrite history, it is true. The minor German Expressionist architect Hermann Finsterlin (1887–1973), whose biomorphic projects of 1919 have lately been cited (erroneously) as a source of inspiration for Frank Gehry's Guggenheim Museum Bilbao of 1991–97, is one noteworthy example. Finsterlin, who long outlived his more important contemporaries, was able to convince credulous authors in the 1960s and 1970s of his purportedly pivotal role in the movement half a century earlier, and thus earned a place in the history books far above his actual accomplishments.[3]

Leaving such considerations aside, there can be no doubt either of Anni Albers's natural affinity for the medium she seemingly stumbled upon or of her primacy among her contemporaries, even while she learned from them. As Hans M. Wingler wrote, "That students learned from each other was more true of the weaving workshop than of any other workshop in the Bauhaus."[4] This reflected Albers's own assertion that "There is this very mistaken idea that there really was an organized course teaching the [weaving] students at that time. Early there wasn't. … What I learned I learned from my co-students."[5]

Thus the high quality of even Albers's earliest works reveals a natural talent for both the craft of weaving and for the intellectual conception of pattern and texture for a flat surface. Her painstakingly detailed renderings for tablecloths and rugs (figs. 3, 4)

are as carefully considered and plotted as a Mondrian canvas, but the finished products invariably display an apparent spontaneity that belies their maker's methodical approach. Indeed, Albers later credited the parameters imposed by her medium as a major factor in freeing her creative instincts: "I find that a craft gives somebody who is trying to find his way a kind of discipline."[6]

Like her husband, Anni Albers was very much influenced by Klee, and her gorgeously multicolored 1925 wall hanging of silk, cotton, and acetate (pl. 5) seems like a homage to the geometric watercolors the master was painting at the time. Albers acknowledged her debt to Klee, but was quick to point out that it was his work, rather than his pedagogy, that had a formative impact on her own artistic development:

What I learned from him I learned from looking at his pictures. Because as a teacher he was not very effective. I sat in a class which he gave to the weaving students and I think I only attended perhaps three of the classes. Klee was so concerned with his own work. He would walk into the room, go up to the blackboard, turn his back to the class, and start to explain something that he probably thought was of concern to those listening to him. But he probably didn't know at all where each of us there was in his own development, in his own concern, in his own searching. I'm sure there were some students who had more direct contact with him. But I didn't have it at all. On the other hand, I find that he probably had more influence on my work and my thinking by just looking at what he did with a line or a dot or a brush stroke and I tried in a way to find my way in my own material and my own craft discipline.[7]

The gradual repositioning of the Bauhaus away from its earlier crafts orientation and toward being a conduit for industrial production—especially after Gropius stepped down as the school's director in 1928 and was replaced by the architect Hannes Meyer—is clearly reflected in Anni Albers's textile designs. As she recalled:

> In the early years, there was a dabbling in a kind of romantic handicraft where you made beautiful pillowcases which—well, you couldn't wash them, perhaps you couldn't sit on them. And these tablecloths in very brilliant and bright colors. But this wasn't what was suited for industry. They couldn't make it in a hundred different threads and colors and so on. And also it wasn't satisfying because it was an over-subjectifying of something that wasn't worth it. When you have a tablecloth that is so active you can't put a plate on that tablecloth, you can't put a vase with flowers on it, it was far too dominating.[8]

She took to heart Klee's admonition that fabrics were "serving objects," and functional considerations began to supersede purely aesthetic concerns. Increasingly her palette changed from the bold colors of her wall hangings of the mid–1920s and toward neutrals and earth tones that had a greater likelihood of commercial success. Though she was unquestionably a gifted colorist, she subordinated that aspect to what she viewed as more important issues:

> In concentrating on what the weaving materials told you, color was almost interfering with this because the roughness, the smoothness, the gloss, et cetera, comes out clearer if you are not concerned with additional color, but if you stick to just what this character of the material was. And therefore, I find that colors in weaving have not the first place, like with a proper painter, but only a secondary one. And if you think of working for industrial production, as I have done to a small degree, a curtain that you build should be—I don't know—transparent, or opaque, folding easily, washable, and so on, and you can have it in blue or red or green in the end, which is a further concern, but it is not the one out of which to build the main character of the material.[9]

Albers loved experimenting with new and unexpected combinations of materials beyond the weaver's conventional wool, cotton, linen, and silk. In the late 1920s she mixed strands of the new packaging wonder cellophane with jute and twisted paper to create an innovative but quite adaptable wall covering (pl. 81), and likewise she was early to use the newly devised rayon and other synthetic fibers for yard goods (pl. 76). After World War II she similarly incorporated plastic in an open-weave fabric that also combined bast fiber, cotton, and horsehair (pl. 110). One of her proudest accomplishments at the Bauhaus—and the scheme that won Albers her diploma in 1930—was a sound-absorbent curtain for the echo-plagued auditorium of Hannes Meyer's ADGB Bundesschule in Bernau. Using cellophane that she unraveled from a cap she bought while on holiday in Italy, she wove the new material with chenille to form a light-reflective wall hanging that effectively deadened the room's acoustic reverberation.

One of Albers's most ingenious applications of her problem-solving skills was the commission she received in 1949 for curtains, bedspreads, and room dividers for the dormitory rooms at the new Harvard Graduate Center, designed by Walter Gropius and his collective firm The Architects' Collaborative. It is difficult to imagine a more punishing environment for soft goods than a college dorm room. But Albers rose to the challenge and devised fabrics that were both sturdy enough to survive the harshest treatment

FIG. 3   ANNI ALBERS   *Design for a tablecloth*, 1930   (detail of pl. 15)

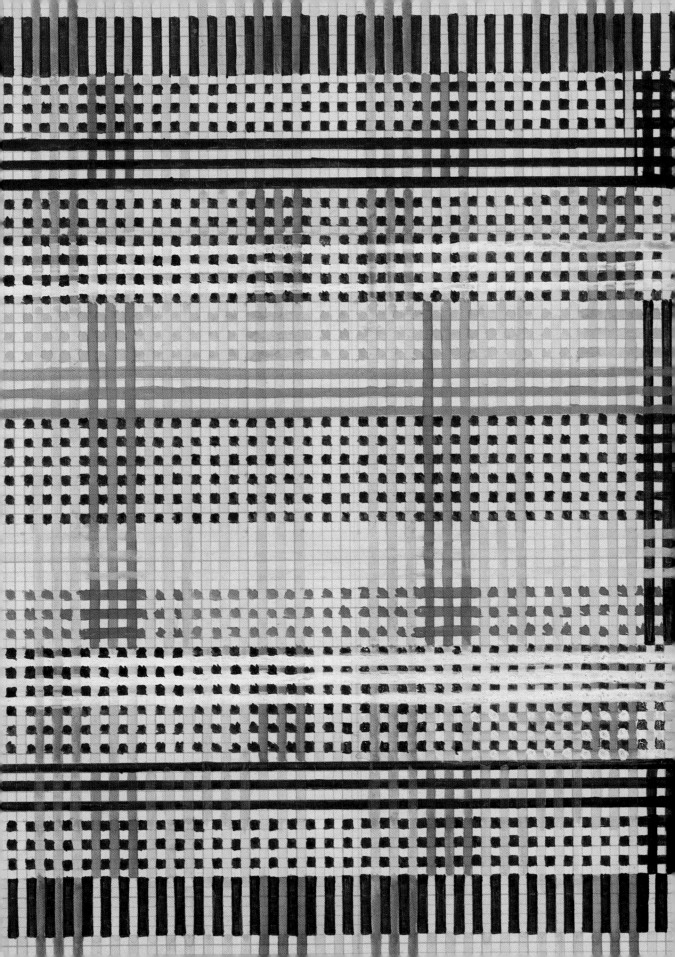

and strongly patterned enough to obscure the stains and other damage they were certain to receive. The heavyweight linen and cotton dividing curtain (pl. 107), with an irregular vertical tan stripe on a black ground, is handsome enough to serve as a wall hanging, but its effectiveness in providing privacy in the dorm's double bedrooms was its designer's primary concern.

Also dating from around 1949 is one of Albers's most ravishing, if atypical, weavings: a free-hanging room divider of cotton, cellophane, and braided horsehair (pl. 100). Its heavy, evenly spaced vertical strips of black braided horsehair are lightly linked with curving openwork strands that bring to mind the tendrils of a plant. As opposed to the Harvard room divider of the same year, this lyrical, sculptural object would do virtually nothing to provide privacy, and it is clearly more decorative than functional. But that its maker could simultaneously shift between such diametrically opposite modes with such ease is just another indication of her virtuosity in a medium by whose conventions she would never be confined.

As members of the first generation of Modernist pioneers, the Alberses were compelled to invent much of their personal environment in order for it to accord with the reductivist aesthetic of the new movement. Before 1926 there were almost no commercially available furnishings that accorded with Bauhaus principles, specifically the emphasis on integrity of structure and material and the prohibition of applied ornament. Like Le Corbusier and Mies van der Rohe, the Alberses had two options in domestic interior design. They either had to find extremely simple vernacular pieces—such as the metal architect's lamp seen in the photograph of their Dessau bedroom— or design them themselves—as with Josef Albers's ash-veneer tea table with a milk-glass top (pl. 55), visible in a photo of the couple's living room.

One of the most influential of all Bauhaus departments was the furniture workshop, from which emerged designs that would transform the interior design of the Modern Movement. Like each of the Bauhaus workshops, it was jointly led by a crafts master, who taught technique, and a form master, who taught design. From 1919 the Expressionist and mystically oriented Johannes Itten served as the form master of what was then called the carpentry workshop. In 1922 Itten was replaced by the rationalist and pragmatist Walter Gropius. After the Bauhaus moved from Weimar to Dessau in 1925, Gropius was in turn succeeded by Marcel Breuer (who had arrived as a student at the Bauhaus shortly after its inception in 1919, and was followed a year later by Josef Albers). The department was renamed the furniture workshop, in recognition of the increasing use being made of metal alongside wood, especially in Breuer's own designs for Thonet, the first commercially produced furniture to emerge from the Bauhaus.

The change in the creative leadership of the carpentry workshop from Itten to Gropius in 1922 had an immediate and extreme effect on the character of the studio's output, dramatically revealed by the furniture displayed at the 1923 Bauhaus exhibition, which confirmed the school's new aesthetic direction. The neo-primitive Expressionist designs produced by Breuer under Itten's influence—such as his high-backed, five-legged African chair of 1921—were supplanted by an entirely new approach, clearly influenced by the abstract reductivism of De Stijl and Russian Constructivism. Although *Bauhäusler* later maintained that claims for De Stijl's influence on the post-Itten school were grossly exaggerated, the chronological and visual evidence indicates otherwise. Writing of Breuer's radical new direction at that time, Christopher Wilk has observed that "the De Stijl influence on his furniture is too strong and too specific to be denied."[10]

FIG. 4 ANNI ALBERS *Design for a jute rug*, 1927 (detail of pl. 10)

The work of De Stijl had been introduced at the Bauhaus by Lyonel Feininger as early as 1919, contemporary with the first publication of Gerrit Rietveld's revolutionary furniture in the Dutch group's eponymous journal. Theo van Doesburg, one of the founders of De Stijl, made several visits to the Bauhaus in the early 1920s. The 1923 Bauhaus exhibition included furniture by Rietveld, whose tubular-bulb hanging lamp of 1920 was the obvious source for the very similar light fixture Gropius devised for his own Weimar Bauhaus office three years later. Furthermore, Rietveld's contribution to the *Greater Berlin Art Exhibition* of 1923—a full-scale model room he designed and furnished in collaboration with the painter Vilmos Huszár—was probably visited by a number of *Bauhäusler*.

Whether Albers saw that remarkably integrated De Stijl environment is not known, but two highly accomplished pieces of furniture that he made that same year show that he had absorbed the ideas of the Dutch movement as skillfully as Breuer had. Albers's *Table for a reception room* from 1923 (pl. 25) suggests that he had closely studied Rietveld's Berlin chair, the centerpiece of the architect–designer's exhibition room. As Daniele Baroni has written of Rietveld's breakthrough reconception of furniture, "It was a method of constructing by planes instead of by lines."[11] Indeed, it can be said of Albers's table, like Rietveld's chair, that it is "like a small building; the legs … were eliminated and replaced by other planes or by asymmetrical structures, free-standing in space and forming a rhythmical pattern and meticulous equilibrium between verticals and horizontals."[12]

Albers's table, intended for the antechamber to the Bauhaus director's office, was described in one photo caption of the period as *aus Brettern konstruiert*— "constructed from boards."[13] That is an accurate but inadequate description, for it is not the vernacular ordinariness of the boards (oak in the original, Baltic birch in the contemporary reproduction) that attracts our attention. Rather, what makes this object extraordinary is the sophisticated composition that Albers creates by joining the four vertical supports— two of which are set on the perpendicular to the others—with three horizontal braces that lightly touch and seem effortlessly to float by them, beneath the broadly overhanging tabletop. To underscore the distinctions between planar elements further, Albers applied a dark stain to the top of all the desk's horizontal parts, much as Rietveld would paint a particular detail in a contrasting or harmonizing value to emphasize or de-emphasize it, depending on the overall coloration of a piece. The resulting effect of Albers's two-tone scheme is at once solidly architectonic and lightly hovering, a tension held in check by the design's faultless proportion and perfect balance.

Also from 1923 is Albers's *Bookshelf/magazine stand* (pl. 29), of both stained and unstained wood, with the horizontal surfaces again dark, and the verticals in the lighter natural finish. Devoid of printed matter on its shelves, the piece projects a strong sculptural quality, quite different from the tubular steel *étagères* by Marcel Breuer visible in the photograph of the Alberses' Dessau living room. Those latter shelves appear merely a material transposition of the traditional library format, whereas the Albers design, with shelves of varying depths seemingly cantilevered out from a central shaft, feels much more dynamic. The piece was meant to be put into commercial production—a promotional brochure for it was printed—but it was never serially manufactured and the original, like that of the *Table for a reception room*, was ultimately lost and presumably destroyed.

Several decorative objects by Albers, albeit with declared utilitarian functions, were made in the mid-1920s as well. These include two versions of a circular silver-plated metal-and-glass fruit bowl resting on three ball feet of ebonized wood (pls. 68, 69). (One example was donated to the Museum of Modern Art by Gropius, to whom it had been given by the designer.) There are also two variants (one dated to 1925) of a heat-resistant clear glass teacup with a porcelain saucer and a circular chromed steel collar affixed with ebony disc handles (pls. 70, 71). The latter relate to tea glasses in silvered bronze holders with ebony handles made by the Bauhaus metal workshop student Max Krajewski a year earlier. Both Krajewski's and Albers's designs refer back to vernacular types common both in Eastern Europe and Russia, where tea is customarily drunk from glass, rather than ceramic, vessels.[14] Albers's teacup differs from Krajewski's in having two handles: a horizontal disc for the server to hand it and a vertical disc for the drinker to receive it, reflecting the designer's belief that a single handle made passing a cup too awkward.

Certainly the most historically significant furniture design by Albers from this period is his laminated plywood armchair of 1926, represented in the following pages by a later variant of 1929 (pl. 43). Anticipating Alvar Aalto's experiments in molded plywood seating from 1929, Albers's scheme, as he wrote, "is, to my knowledge and that of others, the first modern chair in laminated bent wood."[15] How far back in time one wishes to push the parameters of "modern" is open to debate, for Michael Thonet's earliest essays in bentwood furniture, dating to around 1836, are the equivalent of Sir Joseph Paxton's Crystal Palace of 1851, each now considered a founding artifact of Modernism in its respective medium.

Nonetheless, given the long-running debate over who designed the first tubular steel furniture of the 1920s—an innovation now generally attributed to the Dutch architect Mart Stam, with his Thonet armchair of 1925—it seems remarkable that more attention has not been paid to Albers's 1926 armchair.

It is ingeniously constructed from just four wood members: a pair of arms and legs taken from two large lengths of plywood veneers molded over metal forms. The one for the continuous legs and arm rests was bent into an inverted U-shape at angles between 90 and 110 degrees, and the other, to support the seat and chair back, was bent into an angle of about 110 degrees. Both lengths of plywood were then cut, according to Albers's own later diagram (see pl. 48), into equally spaced segments, not unlike slices of a roast or jelly roll.

Albers was particularly proud of the resilience that the two-piece plywood structure gave the design:

This new principle of chair construction has been followed by others in innumerable similar chair productions up to now, but particularly during the thirties and forties.

But I have seen not one that repeats the flexible back of the chair, which, of course, any printed reproduction does not make clearly recognizable.[16]

Why, then, despite its unquestionable significance, does the Albers chair not enjoy higher status in the canon of modern classics? First, it was not manufactured in large enough quantities for it to be widely distributed—and eventually collected, once the Bauhaus had been universally recognized as the most important art and design school of the twentieth century. In purely aesthetic terms, however, it also lacks the iconic power of the best of the many chair designs of Breuer and Mies, to say nothing of those by the *Unbauhäusler* Le Corbusier and particularly Aalto. The Finnish architect's many elegant essays in bent plywood seating, despite Albers's claims, possessed all the "give" of the German's 1926 armchair but presented a far more voluptuous profile, especially when placed in stripped-down International Style interiors.

Yet Albers was clearly on to something when he embraced warm wood rather than cold metal, in contrast to his Bauhaus colleagues who went on to far greater fame as furniture designers with their chrome-plated steel pieces. It was Aalto, with his intuition for organic form and the resources of his country's formidable timber industry behind him, who was able most fully to exploit the potential of the material. In doing so, he made bent plywood an essential element of his humane alternative to the increasingly mechanical character of the International Style in Europe south of Scandinavia.

The limited opportunities to execute modern architectural commissions in Germany during the economically depressed Weimar period led to the proliferation of design exhibitions sponsored by progressive groups to showcase the talents of otherwise underemployed design professionals. Among those shows was the *German Building Exhibition*, held in Berlin in 1931. Albers was but one of its many eminent participants, and his *Living room of an apartment* (fig. 5; pl. 49) at that show summarizes both his strengths and limitations as an interior designer. The model room is furnished with a matching suite of neutral-colored upholstered sofa and three armchairs framed in natural-finish ash, and a circular low table in ash, topped with opaque gray glass. They are set in the narrow rectangular space with a wall of minimally curtained windows to the right, below which is what appears to be a built-in storage unit (though its lack of hardware makes its function, if any, unclear). A rectilinear hanging wall cabinet, faced with sliding panels of apparently the same opaque gray glass as that on the round table, is affixed to the far narrow wall of the room.

This interior seems unusually comfortable by International Style standards, far more welcoming than a stringent Mies or Le Corbusier interior, but it also feels somewhat dull, in the anodyne manner we have come to associate with institutional adaptations of Scandinavian modern designs of the postwar period. The pale, monochromatic color scheme has something to do with this impression, and that lack of contrast, especially in the surviving black-and-white photo of the interior, causes visual interest to flag quickly, as it can do in all but the most rigorously considered International Style room settings.

Far more successful was the large interior commission Albers had undertaken around 1927 for the Berlin home of his friends the psychoanalysts Drs. Fritz and Anna Moellenhoff. This extensive undertaking reveals Josef Albers's extraordinary virtuosity as a designer and places him among the most talented furniture makers of his generation. Here, for clearly sympathetic private clients, he displays a thoughtful inventiveness palpable in almost every piece, and the cumulative effect of these interiors must have been quite impressive.

Among Albers's Moellenhoff designs, fourteen of which are included in the present exhibition, is the severely simple *Sofa in two parts*, an elongated banquette (which seems to float above two narrow wooden supports deeply inset from the ends of the piece), and a matching square *Ottoman* (pls. 37, 38). Also presumably used in the living room was an *Armchair* (pl. 42), the sides of which are framed with large outlined squares of wood, with the back and seat suspended at a tilted right angle within them. This format reflects the approximate proportions of Breuer's well-known Club armchair of late 1927 or early 1928 (commonly known as the Wassily chair), two early prototypes of which can be seen in the 1928 photograph of the Alberses' Dessau living room.

The dining room of the Moellenhoff house was dominated by a large sideboard of walnut with maple veneer, ebonized fruitwood detailing, and panels of frosted glass. Its lively, asymmetrical composition was undermined when at some point the piece was sawn

FIG. 5 JOSEF ALBERS *Living room of an apartment for the German Building Exhibition, Berlin, 1931* (detail of pl. 49)

through the middle, no doubt to make it easier to move. Though the parts have now been rejoined, the sideboard's still-visible breaks make it more difficult to read as a continuous whole. If the ample *Büfett* was a staple of the properly furnished *bürgerlich* dining room (even the revolutionary Rietveld designed one), then the *Schrank*, or armoire, was an equally standard component of the middle-class German bedroom.

The massive walnut and maple *Double armoire* (fig. 6; pl. 36) that Albers created for the Moellenhoffs demonstrates his ability to infuse even the most mundane of storage units with unusual interest. Here he divides the piece vertically into two equal portions, and then subdivides them with an identical series of doors concealing shelves and hanging space behind them. By slightly recessing the darker walnut surfaces that form inverted L-shapes and frame the lighter maple paneling of the largest doors, Albers sets up a repetitive asymmetry that agreeably breaks down the bulk of what otherwise would have been a dauntingly monolithic object.

When the Moellenhoffs immigrated to the United States after Hitler's rise to power (like the Alberses, the husband was Christian and the wife Jewish), they took their Albers furniture with them, and reinstalled it in their first American home at Black Mountain College, North Carolina, and later in their apartment in Chicago. This represents a rare survival of a major custom-furniture installation of the Weimar period, as a number of such avant-garde commissions—many of them initiated by Jewish clients—were lost in the coming maelstrom. (Restrictions on what Jews could take with them from Germany were gradually tightened throughout the 1930s. By 1938, the Hitler regime had prohibited Jews from departing with any financial instruments, and refugees sometimes resorted to converting cash into household goods—especially antiques—that might be sold when they

reached their destination.) Few of those furnishings, however, were as representative of Germany's unparalleled contribution to modern design as the Moellenhoff commission, which deserves greater recognition in the history of modern design in Germany during its fifteen-year *Goldene Zeit* before Hitler's ascendance.

Among the most fascinating and successful subsections within Anni Albers's overall œuvre is the jewelry she produced in collaboration with Alex Reed, a student and later teacher at Black Mountain College in North Carolina, where the Alberses taught from 1933 until 1949. As Anni Albers wrote in 1942:

> The first stimulus to make jewelry from hardware came to us from the treasure of Monte Alban, the most precious jewels from ancient Mexico, found only a few years ago in a tomb near Oaxaca. These objects of gold and pearls, of jade, rock-crystal, and shells, made about 1,000 years ago, are of such surprising beauty in unusual combinations of materials that we became aware of the strange limitations in materials commonly used for jewels today. ... [B]ack in the States, we looked for new materials to use. In the 5 & 10 cents stores we discovered the beauty of washers and bobby-pins. Enchanted we stood before kitchen-sink stoppers and glass insulators, picture hooks and erasers. The art of Monte Alban had given us the freedom to see things detached from their use, as pure materials, worth being turned into precious objects.[17]

In this respect Albers and Reed were reflecting the Modernist fascination with vernacular industrial design as found art objects, exemplified by Philip Johnson's 1934 Museum of Modern Art exhibition *Machine Art*, in which ball bearings and propellers were placed on pedestals and elevated to the status of

FIG. 6 JOSEF ALBERS *Double armoire, c.* 1927 (detail of pl. 36)

high sculpture. (Josef Albers designed the powerfully graphic cover for the show's catalog, a year after Johnson and his Harvard contemporary Edward M.M. Warburg brought the Alberses to America; see pl. 75.)[18] Johnson, in turn, had obviously been inspired by the Dadaists' earlier and more audacious appropriation and transformation of functional objects, in which they removed them from their original contexts and deemed them, perforce, to be art. That strategy was most famously epitomized by Marcel Duchamp's celebrated "ready-mades": *Bicycle Wheel* of 1913, *Bottlerack* of 1914, *In Advance of the Broken Arm* of 1915 (a snow shovel), and *Fountain* of 1917 (a urinal).

Albers' and Reed's playful recombinations of everyday utilitarian devices into a series of arresting necklaces—a perforated aluminum drain strainer festooned with a fringe of paper clips and suspended from a ball-link chain (pl. 118); aluminum washers (pls. 119, 120) and brass grommets (pl. 121) strung on grosgrain ribbon or a chamois strip; and bobby pins spaced along a ball-link chain (fig. 7; pl. 117), all *c*. 1940—fall somewhere between the anarchic approach of Duchamp and the aestheticized response of Johnson. The strainer necklace in particular evokes the flat planar juxtaposition of humble objects in strong silhouette typical of the 1920s photograms of László Moholy-Nagy, which Albers had undoubtedly seen at the Bauhaus during Moholy-Nagy's tenure. And this pendant likewise brings to mind the stylized natural motifs of Southwest American Indian jewelry: the strainer as solar disc, perhaps, or the suspended paper clips as the tail feathers of an eagle. Intentional or not, such references only enhance the sly wit of these delightful artifacts.

Tellingly, Albers' and Reed's finished jewelry never seems as overtly machine-like as its component parts would suggest. Some pieces, especially the brass chokers, have a distinctly Pre-Columbian feel: both the color and shape of the grommets recall Mayan gold beads. A more contemporaneous comparison can be made with the jewelry designs of Alexander Calder, for although Calder's similarly bold but clearly handcrafted forms were individually rather than industrially made, those designs also occasionally incorporated *objets trouvés* such as small bones, uncut stones, and pieces of colored glass. However, the abstracted natural forms that Calder came to by way of Surrealism were quite different from the non-representational character of the Albers–Reed ornaments.

No medium better conveys Josef Albers's comprehensive commitment to the Modernist sensibility than his work in graphic design. Though not extensive, his typographic efforts over more than half a century retain an immediacy that bespeaks his evolving yet always consistent aesthetic. At the Bauhaus, Albers invented a highly individualized font, his "universal typeface" of *c*. 1926 (fig. 8; pl. 74). Developed on paper scored with a tiny grid, this stylized alphabet is composed of recombinations of ten elements, only two of which are rectilinear, with all the others partially curved. As display lettering it is striking, if not particularly legible—the "c" and "v" are both difficult to decipher—and it brings to mind the eccentric typographic experiments of the contemporaneous Amsterdam School, the Dutch Expressionist counterpart of the De Stijl movement. The fact that Albers's universal typeface never became anything approaching universal in its application says something about its inherent functional shortcomings.

Albers's most personal expressions in graphic design were the Christmas cards he began producing after arriving in the United States in 1933 and continued to create over the ensuing decades. Although his 1934 greeting was typeset, the choice of font is clearly designed to evoke the "construction

FIG. 7 ANNI ALBERS *Necklace, c.* 1940 (detail of pl. 117)

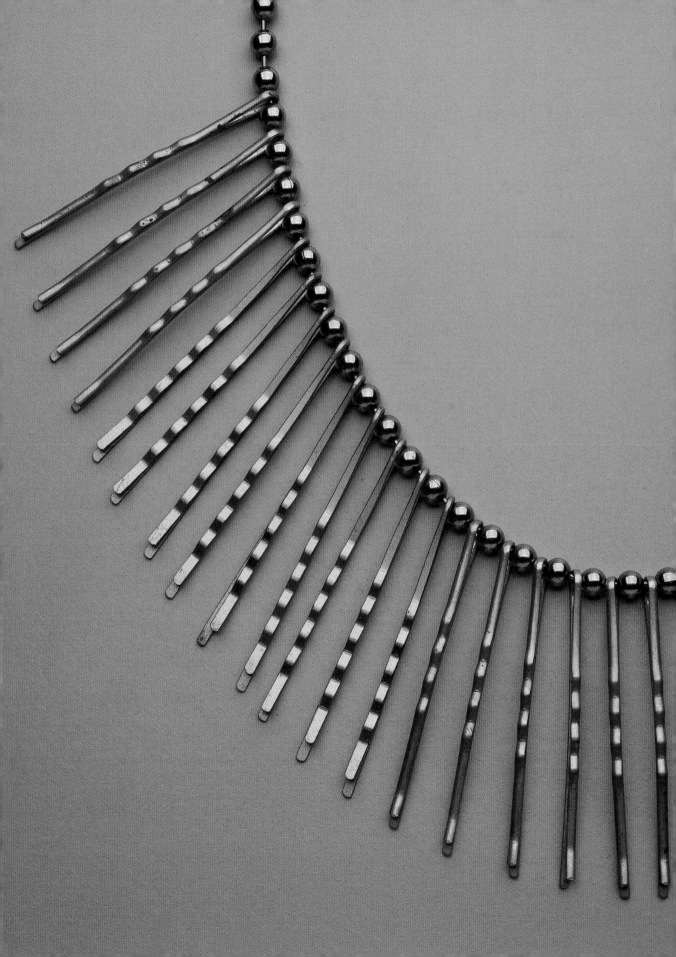

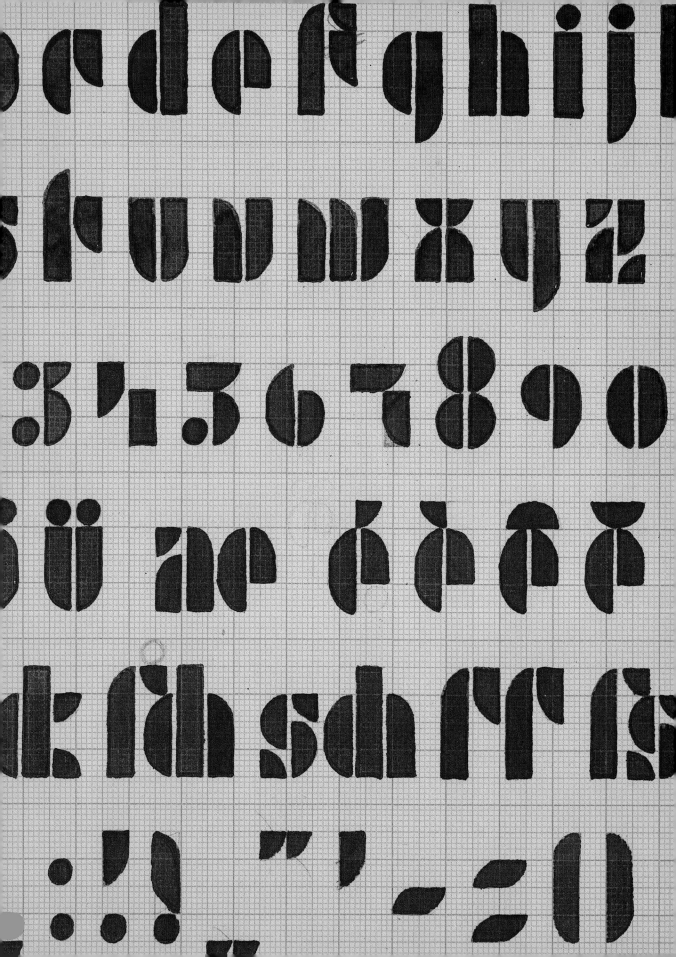

exercises" he assigned his Bauhaus students, in which he instructed them to use the typewriter as an instrument for making pictures—a technique that had been employed by professional typists since at least the 1890s. Here the text reads "A MERRY CHRISTMAS AND A HAPPY NEW YEAR" over and over again in three columns (pl. 122). The words of the center column are underlined to heighten the graphic effect but were not organized into an overall geometric pattern, as were the original typewriter exercises published in the Bauhaus magazine edited by Gropius.

In 1939 Albers took another approach to the found object by appropriating colored picture postcards of "the Loop," a curving road near Newfound Gap in Great Smoky Mountains National Park, which he bought on a break there from Black Mountain College. Because that aerial view of "the Loop" made it look like a gigantic "3", Albers painted a matching "9" next to it and stenciled two words at an angle above the altered image so that the greeting read "a good 39" (pl. 123). He was so intrigued by the idea that he used another overhead view of "the Loop" for his 1943 greeting (pl. 127).

There is no known complete collection of Albers Christmas cards, but the gridded black-and-white 1950 design (pl. 128)—concluding the year in which the artist began his *Homage to the Square* series at the age of sixty-two—marks a definite departure from his Surreal imagery of the 1940s. The 1952 card (pl. 130) is an exercise in *Gestalt* perception—the human ability to mentally complete visually incomplete forms—that had intrigued both *Bauhäusler* and members of De Stijl three decades earlier. Here Albers sets up a grid of white dots offset against a black background, eliminating them at symmetrical points, so that when viewed as a whole the negative pattern reads as a multiple quatrefoil, Greek cross, or stylized snowflake.

Gestalt perception was exploited in several of the excellent record album covers that Albers designed in the 1950s and 1960s for Command Records, including those for the *Persuasive Percussion* and *Provocative Percussion* series, performed by Enoch Light and the Light Brigade. (Their best-selling LPs of heavily percussive big-band arrangements were favorites of the period's high-fidelity buffs, who used them to show off the acoustic capabilities of their new stereo sound systems.) Albers aptly captured the essence of the not-so-light Light touch with boldly graphic covers that looked the way the records sounded, with simple geometric shapes strongly silhouetted against a solid background—a kind of visual onomatopoeia.

The first *Persuasive Percussion* design, of 1959 (pl. 136), featured regular columns of black dots on a white field, with a single dot from each column pulled up toward the top of the composition and arranged in an uneven row like abstracted musical notation. Equally evocative of classical music was Albers's scheme for the Command recording of Ravel's orchestration of Mussorgsky's *Pictures at an Exhibition* (pl. 141). Against the album cover's black background, thin white vertical lines were broken by five differently proportioned rectangular voids that implied a row of paintings on a wall, a *Gestalt* summarization of the composer's tone poem.

Although Albers was preoccupied during his last quarter century with painting, he would still turn to design projects from time to time when a proposal captured his imagination. One such occasion came when he was asked by the architect King-lui Wu, a colleague on the faculty at Yale, where Josef headed the Department of Design, to contribute a fireplace design to Wu's Rouse house of 1955 in North Haven, Connecticut (pl. 147). The chimneypiece, made of off-white firebrick, is a virtuoso demonstration of Albers's ability to take a humble material and to develop it into a highly sophisticated artifact.

FIG. 8 JOSEF ALBERS *Design for a universal typeface, c. 1926* (detail of pl. 74)

The many small wooden study models that Albers made to work out this forcefully sculptural hearth betray the thoroughness with which he approached what some other artists might have considered a minor decorative commission. But as with everything he undertook, Albers turned the full force of his artistic intelligence to the task at hand, and treated the fireplace as seriously as a large-scale sculpture. As Albers's Rouse fireplace maquettes show, he debated long and hard as to how the rhythmic angling of the bricks could be used to best advantage. The carefully considered play of light and shadow over the faceted surface of the chimneypiece was in consonance with Wu's belief that light is the "most noble of natural phenomena," which he made the subject of his long-running course "Daylight and Architecture" at the Yale School of Architecture.[19]

The expressive brickwork common to German Expressionist architecture (such as Fritz Höger's Chilehaus of 1923 in Hamburg) and the work of the Amsterdam School (including Michel de Klerk's Eigen Haard housing of 1917–21 in Amsterdam) suggest obvious prototypes. And Albers's particular handling of the light-colored brick is also reminiscent of Alvar Aalto's interestingly textured brick and ceramic-tile wall surfaces after he moved beyond his purist International Style phase in the mid-1930s. There is no more elemental symbol of the home than the hearth, and here Albers invests it with a commanding presence that sums up his and Anni Albers's extraordinary ability to restate age-old truths in a timelessly modern idiom, a hallmark of their entire, and still vibrant, body of design.

NOTES

1   Rosemarie Haag Bletter, "The Interpretation of the Glass Dream: Expressionist Architecture and the History of the Crystal Metaphor" in *The Light Construction Reader*, ed. Todd Gannon, New York (Monacelli Press) 2002, pp. 311–35. For a more condensed and updated discussion of the subject, see Bletter, "Mies and Dark Transparency" in Terence Riley and Barry Bergdoll, *Mies in Berlin*, New York (Museum of Modern Art/Harry N. Abrams) 2001, pp. 350–57.

2   Anni Albers, interview conducted by Sevim Fesci at New Haven CT for the Archives of American Art, The Smithsonian Institution, July 5, 1968.

3   Dennis Sharp, *Modern Architecture and Expressionism*, New York (George Braziller) 1966. F. Borsi and G.K. König, *Architettura dell'Expressionismo*, Genoa (Vitali e Ghianda) and Paris (Vincent, Freal et Cie) 1972.

4   Hans M. Wingler, *The Bauhaus: Weimar Dessau Berlin*, Cambridge MA and London (MIT Press) 1969, p. 461.

5   Albers, *op. cit.*

6   *Ibid.*

7   *Ibid.*

8   *Ibid.*

9   *Ibid.*

10 Christopher Wilk, *Marcel Breuer: Furniture and Interiors*, New York (Museum of Modern Art) 1981, p. 26.

11 Daniele Baroni, *The Furniture of Gerrit Thomas Rietveld*, Woodbury NY (Barron's) 1978, p. 84.

12 *Ibid.*

13 Gustav Adolf Platz, *Wohnräume der Gegenwart*, Berlin (Propyläen Verlag) 1933, p. 445.

14 Herbert Bayer, Walter Gropius, and Ise Gropius (eds.), *Bauhaus: 1919–1928*, New York (Museum of Modern Art) 1938, p. 53.

15 Josef Albers, typewritten sheet with blue ballpoint pen drawing of "My armchair of 1926 …", n.d., The Josef and Anni Albers Foundation.

16 *Ibid.*

17 Anni Albers, "On Jewelry," in *Anni Albers: Selected Writings on Design*, ed. Brenda Danilowitz, Hanover and London (University Press of New England) 2000, pp. 22–23.

18 Philip Johnson (ed.), *Machine Art*, March 6 to April 30, 1934, New York (Museum of Modern Art) 1934.

19 David W. Dunlap, "King-lui Wu, 84, Architect and Longtime Yale Professor," *New York Times*, August 25, 2002, p. 31.

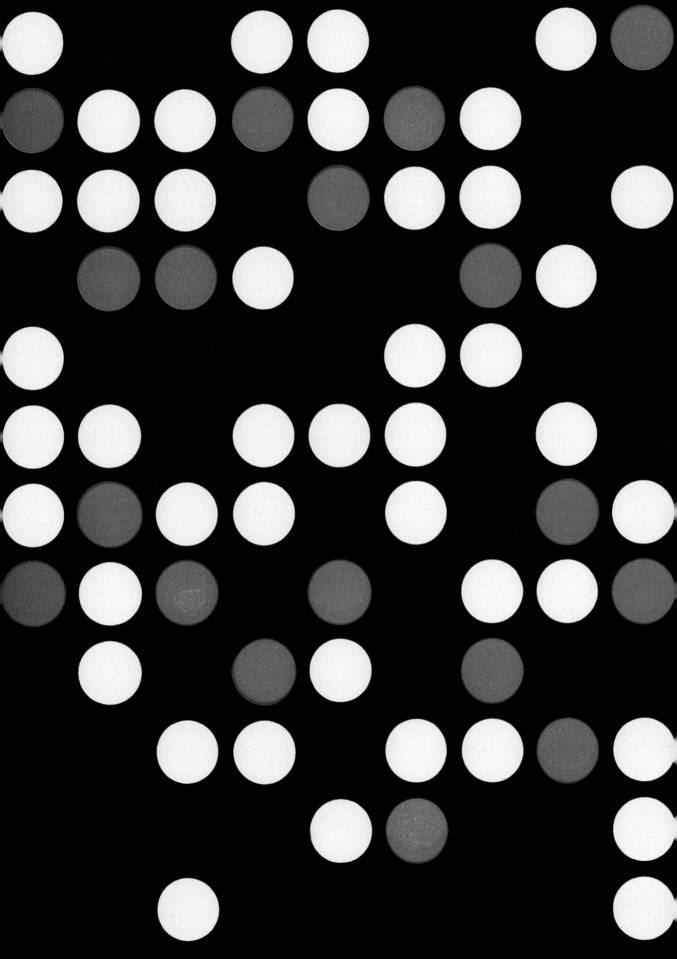

THE WORKS OF JOSEF AND ANNI ALBERS

(previous page)
Anni and Josef, Black Mountain College, c. 1928.
Photograph by Ted Dreier

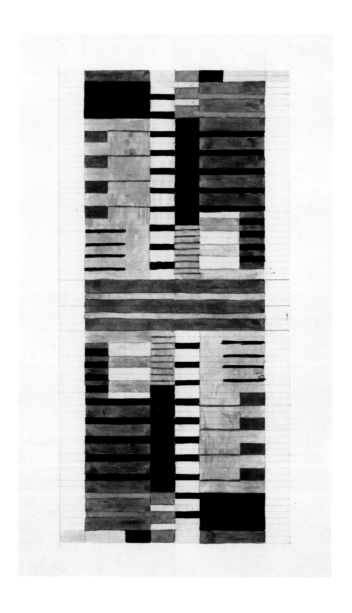

1 ANNI ALBERS
Design for a silk tapestry, 1925
Watercolor and gouache over graphite on
off-white wove paper
11 ¾ × 8 ¾ ins (29.7 × 22.1 cm)
Cambridge MA, Busch-Reisinger Museum, Harvard
University Art Museums, Gift of Anni Albers

2 ANNI ALBERS
Design for a tapestry, 1925
Watercolor and gouache over graphite on
heavy cream wove paper
22 ½ × 10 ¼ ins (57.2 × 26 cm)
Cambridge MA, Busch-Reisinger Museum, Harvard
University Art Museums, Gift of Anni Albers

3 ANNI ALBERS
Design for a Smyrna rug, 1925
Watercolor, gouache, and graphite on paper
8 ⅛ × 6 ½ ins (20.6 × 16.7 cm)
New York, Museum of Modern Art,
Gift of the designer

4 ANNI ALBERS
Design for a jacquard weaving, 1926
Watercolor and gouache over graphite on
heavy cream wove paper
13 ½ × 11 ¼ ins (34.3 × 28.6 cm)
Cambridge MA, Busch-Reisinger Museum, Harvard
University Art Museums, Gift of Anni Albers

5 ANNI ALBERS
Wall hanging, 1925
Silk, cotton, and acetate
57 ⅛ × 36 ¼ ins (145 × 92 cm)
Munich, Die Neue Sammlung, Staatliches
Museum für Angewandte Kunst

6 ANNI ALBERS
Wall hanging, 1925
Wool and silk
92 ⅞ × 37 ¾ ins (236 × 96 cm)
Munich, Die Neue Sammlung, Staatliches
Museum für Angewandte Kunst

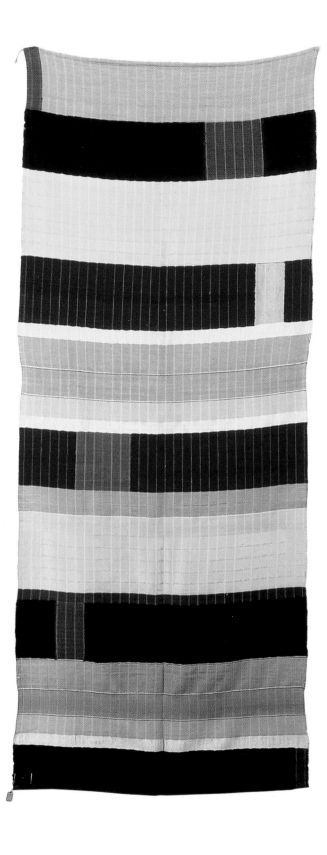

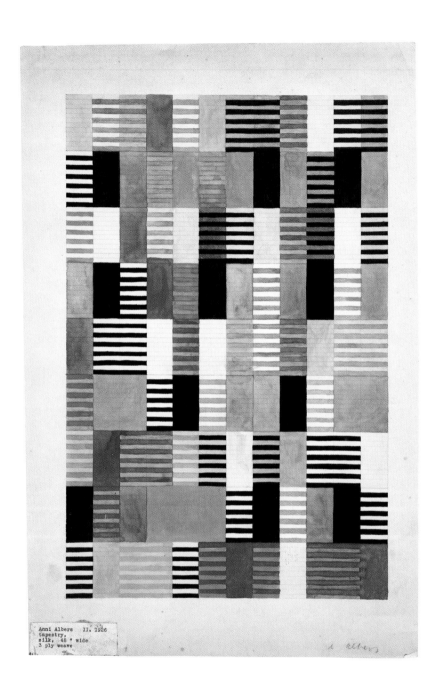

7 ANNI ALBERS
Design for a silk tapestry, 1926
Watercolor and gouache over graphite on
heavy cream wove paper
18 ⅞ × 12 ½ ins (47.8 × 31.7 cm)
Cambridge MA, Busch-Reisinger Museum, Harvard
University Art Museums, Gift of Anni Albers

8 ANNI ALBERS
Wall hanging, 1926
Silk
72 × 48 ins (182.9 × 122 cm)
Cambridge MA, Busch-Reisinger Museum, Harvard
University Art Museums, Association Fund

9 ANNI ALBERS
Design for a rug, 1927
Black ink and watercolor over graphite with collage
elements on white wove paper with collage elements
12 ⅜ × 9 ⅞ ins (32.1 × 25.1 cm)
Cambridge MA, Busch-Reisinger Museum, Harvard
University Art Museums, Gift of Anni Albers

10 ANNI ALBERS
Design for a jute rug, 1927
Watercolor and India ink on paper
13 ⅜ × 10 ⅜ ins (34.6 × 26.3 cm)
New York, Museum of Modern Art,
Gift of the designer

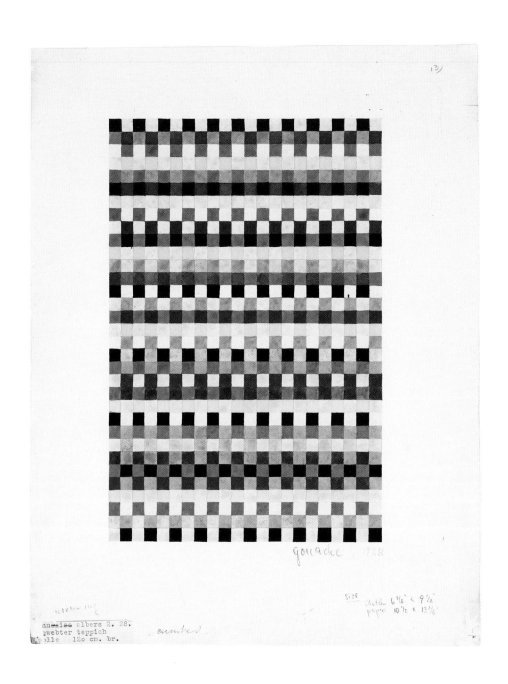

11 ANNI ALBERS
Design for a rug for a child's room, 1928
Gouache on paper
13 ⅜ × 10 ½ ins (34.1 × 26.5 cm)
New York, Museum of Modern Art,
Gift of the designer

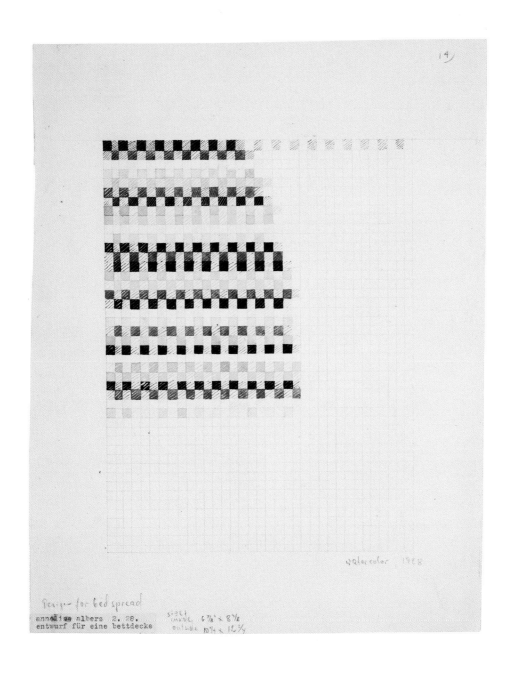

12 ANNI ALBERS
Design for a bedspread, 1928
Watercolor and pencil on paper
12 ³⁄₄ × 10 ¹⁄₄ ins (32.5 × 25.9 cm)
New York, Museum of Modern Art,
Gift of the designer

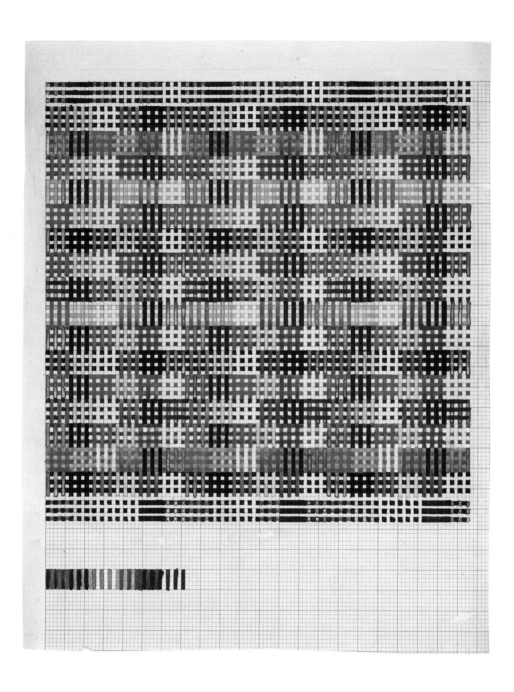

13 ANNI ALBERS
Design for a tablecloth, 1930
Gouache on paper
11 ⅞ × 9 ⅜ ins (30.2 × 23.8 cm)
New York, Museum of Modern Art,
Gift of the designer

14 ANNI ALBERS
Tablecloth fabric sample, 1930
Mercerized cotton
28 ½ × 23 ⅜ ins (72.4 × 59.3 cm)
New York, Museum of Modern Art, Purchase Fund

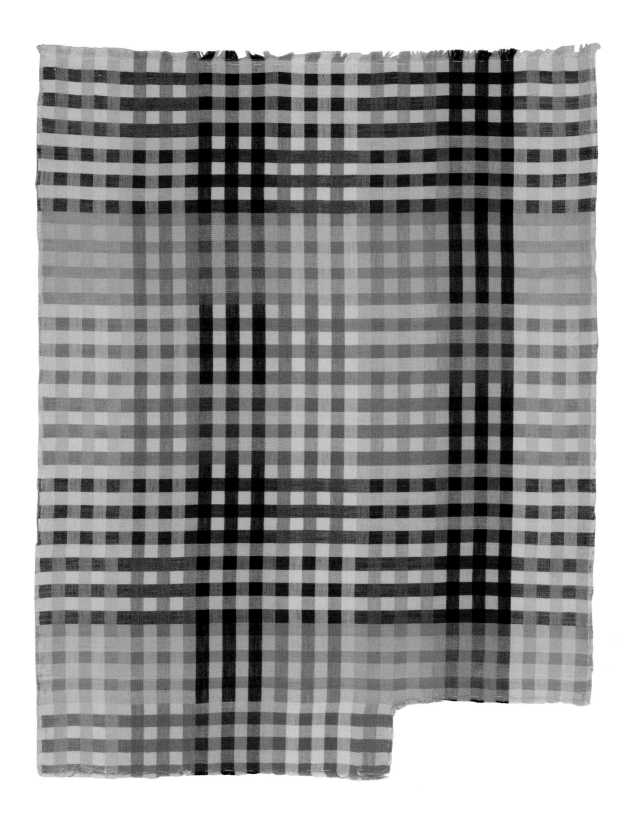

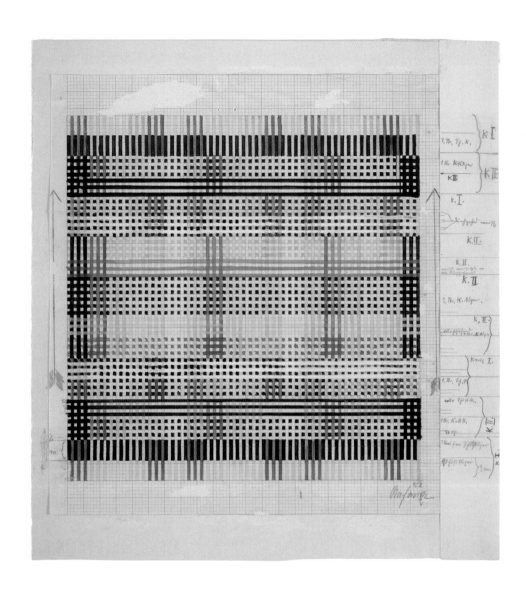

15 ANNI ALBERS
Design for a tablecloth, 1930
Watercolor and gouache on square-ruled paper
10 ¼ × 9 ½ ins (26 × 24.1 cm)
New York, Museum of Modern Art,
Gift of the designer

16 ANNI ALBERS
Drawing for Rug II, 1959
Gouache on paper
5 ⅛ × 17 ⅛ ins (13.1 × 43.6 cm)
Bethany CT, The Josef and Anni Albers Foundation

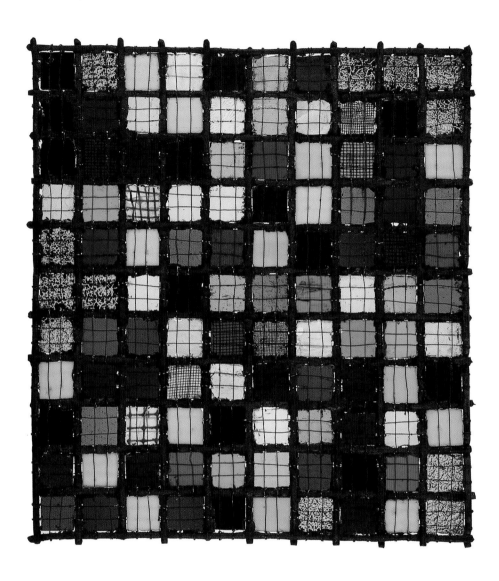

17 JOSEF ALBERS
Grid Picture, 1921
Glass pieces interlaced with copper wire, in a
sheet of fence latticework
12 ¾ × 11 ⅜ ins (32.4 × 28.9 cm)
Bethany CT, The Josef and Anni Albers Foundation

18 JOSEF ALBERS
Untitled, 1921
Glass, wire, and metal, in a metal frame
14 ¾ × 11 ¾ ins (37.5 × 29.8 cm)
Bethany CT, The Josef and Anni Albers Foundation

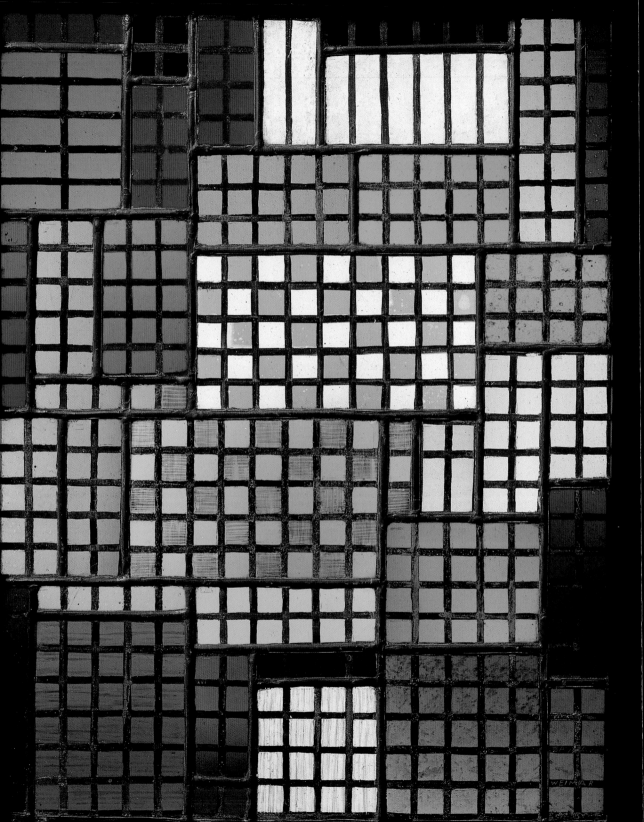

19 JOSEF ALBERS
Park, c. 1924
Glass, wire, metal, and paint, in a wooden frame
19 ½ × 15 ins (49.5 × 38 cm)
Bethany CT, The Josef and Anni Albers Foundation

20 JOSEF ALBERS
Skyscrapers on Transparent Yellow, c. 1929
Sandblasted glass with black paint
13 ⅞ × 13 ¾ ins (35.2 × 34.9 cm)
Bethany CT, The Josef and Anni Albers Foundation

21 JOSEF ALBERS
Goldrosa, *c*. 1926
Sandblasted flashed glass with black paint
17 ½ × 12 ⅜ ins (44.6 × 31.4 cm)
Bethany CT, The Josef and Anni Albers Foundation

22 JOSEF ALBERS
Upward, *c.* 1926
Sandblasted flashed glass with black paint
17 ½ × 12 ⅜ ins (44.6 × 31.4 cm)
Bethany CT, The Josef and Anni Albers Foundation

23 JOSEF ALBERS
Interior (a), 1929
Sandblasted opaque flashed glass
10 × 8 ½ ins (25.6 × 21.4 cm)
Bethany CT, The Josef and Anni Albers Foundation

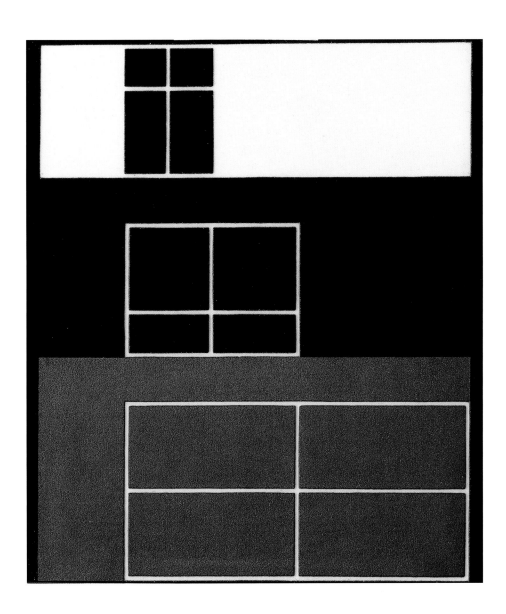

24 JOSEF ALBERS
Interior (b), 1929
Sandblasted opaque flashed glass
10 × 8 ½ ins (25.6 × 21.4 cm)
Bethany CT, The Josef and Anni Albers Foundation

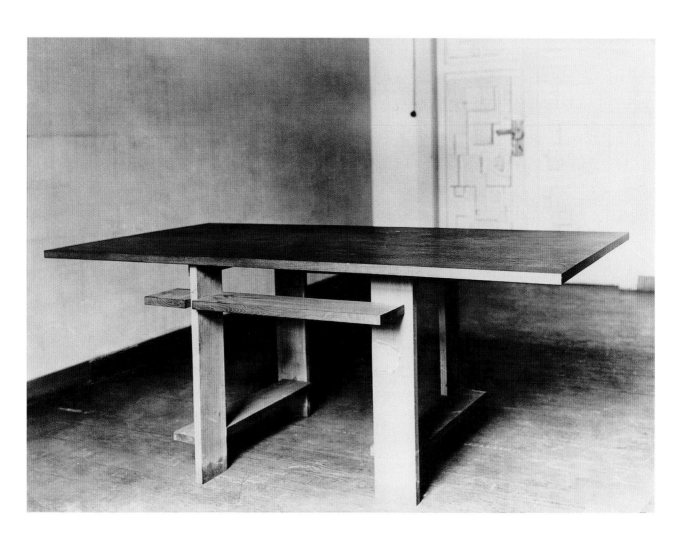

(above)
25 JOSEF ALBERS
Table for a reception room, 1923
Oak (destroyed)
Dimensions unknown

(opposite)
26 JOSEF ALBERS
Table for a reception room, 1923
Baltic birch, reproduction by Rupert Deese (1999),
based on a photograph of the destroyed original
24 ⅝ × 68 ⅜ × 34 ⅛ ins (62.5 × 173.7 × 86.7 cm)
Bethany CT, The Josef and Anni Albers Foundation

(right)
27 JOSEF ALBERS
Exhibition display case of oak and glass for the 1923
Bauhaus Exhibition, 1923
Gelatin silver print
Berlin, Bauhaus-Archiv

gesch.
Höhe 140 cm
Breite 140 cm
Tiefe 35 cm
AUSFÜHRUNG

Zweifarbiges Holz
wagerechte Teile dunkel
senkrechte Teile hell

TI
8

ZEITSCHRIFTEN- UND NOTENREGAL

VORTEILE

1 bequeme Handhabung, da seitlich offen
2 Übersichtlichkeit, da durch die größeren freien Flächen die
   einzelnen Fächer heller sind

Beju 10

28 *Page from Bauhaus GmbH sample catalogue, 1925,*
showing Josef Albers's Bookshelf/magazine stand
of 1923
Berlin, Bauhaus-Archiv

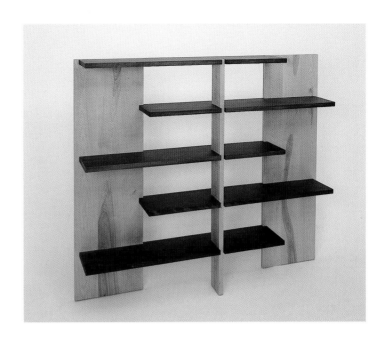

(top)
29 JOSEF ALBERS
Bookshelf/magazine stand, 1923
Baltic birch, reproduction by Rupert Deese (1999)
based on a photograph of the destroyed original
57 ⅛ × 68 ⅜ × 11 ⅜ ins (145.1 × 173.7 × 28.9 cm)
Bethany CT, The Josef and Anni Albers Foundation

(above left)
30 JOSEF ALBERS AND MARCEL BREUER
Library in Wissinger House, Berlin, 1925–26
Gelatin silver print
Berlin, Bauhaus-Archiv

31 JOSEF ALBERS
Set of four stacking tables, *c.* 1927
Ash veneer, black lacquer, and painted glass
15 ⅝ × 16 ½ × 15 ¾ ins (39.7 × 41.9 × 40 cm);
18 ⅝ × 18 ⅞ × 15 ¾ ins (47.3 × 47.9 × 40 cm);
21 ¾ × 21 × 15 ¾ ins (55.2 × 53.5 × 40 cm);
24 ⅝ × 23 ⅝ × 15 ⅞ ins (62.5 × 60 × 40.3 cm)
Bethany CT, The Josef and Anni Albers Foundation, Gift of John and Andrea Weil in memory of Fritz and Anna Moellenhoff

(right)

32 JOSEF ALBERS
Writing desk, *c*. 1927
Ash veneer, black lacquer, and painted glass
30 × 35 ⅜ × 23 ins (76.2 × 89.8 × 58.9 cm)
[with leaf extended: 30 × 52 ¼ × 23 ins
(76.2 × 127.6 × 58.9 cm)]
New York, Collection of Esther M. English

(below)

33 JOSEF ALBERS
Office desk, *c*. 1927
Ash and mahogany, black lacquer
30 × 62 × 30 ins (76.2 × 157.5 × 76.2 cm)
Bethany CT, The Josef and Anni Albers
Foundation, Gift of John and Andrea Weil in
memory of Fritz and Anna Moellenhoff

34 JOSEF ALBERS
Hanging shelf, c. 1927
Wood, ash, and fruitwood
16 ½ × 19 ¾ × 6 ⅞ ins (41.9 × 50.2 × 17.4 cm),
Chicago, The Art Institute of Chicago, Bequest of
Dr. Fritz Moellenhoff and Dr. Anna Moellenhoff

35 JOSEF ALBERS
Bedroom stool, c. 1927
Walnut with horsehair upholstery
16 ⅜ × 16 ½ × 14 ins (42.2 × 41.9 × 35.6 cm)
Bethany CT, The Josef and Anni Albers
Foundation, Gift of John and Andrea Weil in
memory of Fritz and Anna Moellenhoff

36 JOSEF ALBERS
Double armoire, c. 1927
Walnut and maple
74 ¾ × 135 ½ × 19 ½ ins (189.9 × 344.2 × 49.5 cm)
Bethany CT, The Josef and Anni Albers
Foundation, Gift of John and Andrea Weil in
memory of Fritz and Anna Moellenhoff

37 JOSEF ALBERS
Sofa in two parts
(a) Sofa, c. 1927
Walnut and maple veneers with horsehair
upholstery
19 × 75 ½ × 31 ¼ ins (48.3 × 191.8 × 79.4 cm)
Chicago, The Art Institute of Chicago, Bequest of
Dr. Fritz Moellenhoff and Dr. Anna Moellenhoff

38 JOSEF ALBERS
Sofa in two parts
(b) Ottoman, c. 1927
Walnut and maple veneers with horsehair
upholstery
26 × 27 ½ × 24 ¼ ins (66 × 69.8 × 61.6 cm)
Chicago, The Art Institute of Chicago, Bequest of
Dr. Fritz Moellenhoff and Dr. Anna Moellenhoff

39 JOSEF ALBERS
Sideboard, c. 1927
Wood, walnut and maple veneers, ebonized
fruitwood, woven fabric, and horsehair
47 ⅞ × 99 ⅜ × 19 ⅝ ins (121.7 × 252.8 × 49.8 cm)
Chicago, The Art Institute of Chicago, Bequest of
Dr. Fritz Moellenhoff and Dr. Anna Moellenhoff

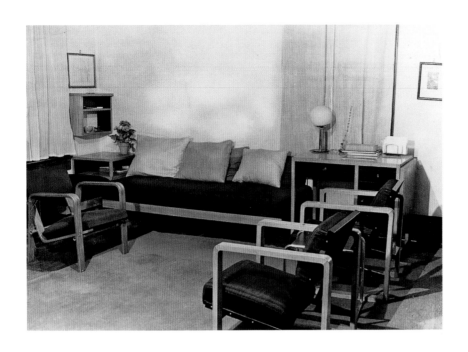

40 *Drs. Fritz and Anna Moellenhoff's living room,*
Black Mountain College, c. 1938
Gelatin silver print
Raleigh NC, North Carolina Office of Archives
and History

41 JOSEF ALBERS
Corner table, c. 1927
Ash
23 ³/₈ × 19 ¹/₂ × 19 ¹/₂ ins (60 × 49.7 × 49.7 cm)
Chicago, The Art Institute of Chicago, Bequest of
Dr. Fritz Moellenhoff and Dr. Anna Moellenhoff

42 JOSEF ALBERS

Armchair, c. 1927
*W*ood, elm, walnut, and maple veneers, ebonized
fruit wood, woven fabric, and horsehair
28 ½ × 24 ⅛ × 25 ¼ ins (72.5 × 61.3 × 64.2 cm)
Chicago, The Art Institute of Chicago, Bequest of
Dr. Fritz Moellenhoff and Dr. Anna Moellenhoff

(opposite)
43 JOSEF ALBERS
Armchair, 1929
Laminated ash, tubular steel, and fabric upholstery
28 ½ × 23 × 28 ½ ins (72.4 × 58.4 × 72.4 cm)
Bethany CT, The Josef and Anni Albers Foundation

(right)
44 JOSEF ALBERS
Design for an armchair, c. 1928
Pencil on paper
33 × 27 ½ ins (83.7 × 69.8 cm)
Bethany CT, The Josef and Anni Albers Foundation

(below)
45 JOSEF ALBERS
Armchair for Dr. Oeser, Berlin, 1928
Walnut and maplewood veneer with fabric
upholstery
29 ⅛ × 24 ¼ × 26 ½ ins (74 × 61.5 × 67.4 cm)
Berlin, Bauhaus-Archiv

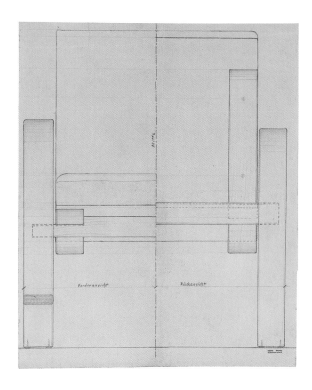

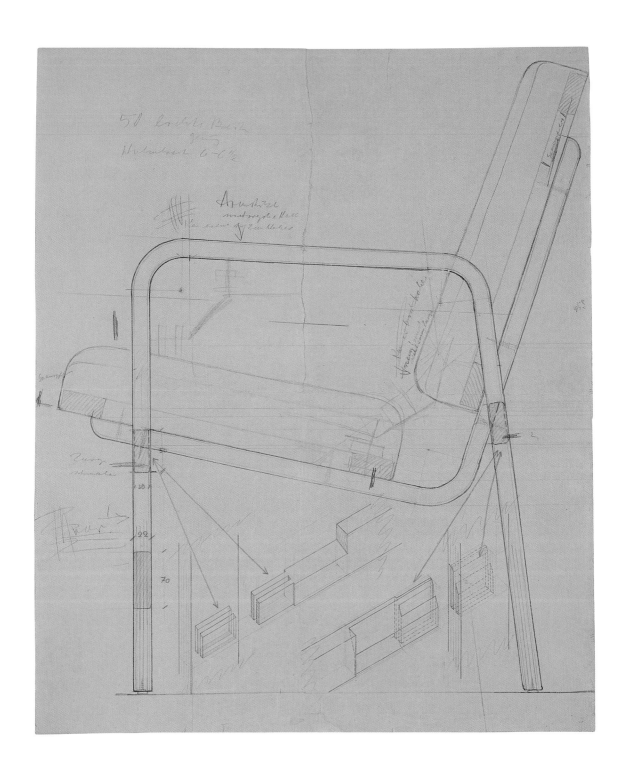

46 JOSEF ALBERS
Design for an armchair, c. 1929
Pencil on paper
33 × 27 ½ ins (83.7 × 69.8 cm)
Bethany CT, The Josef and Anni Albers Foundation

47 JOSEF ALBERS
Armchair, model ti 244, 1929
Laminated beechwood, tubular steel,
and canvas upholstery
28 ½ × 23 × 28 ½ ins (72.4 × 58.9 × 72.4 cm)
New York, Museum of Modern Art,
Gift of the designer

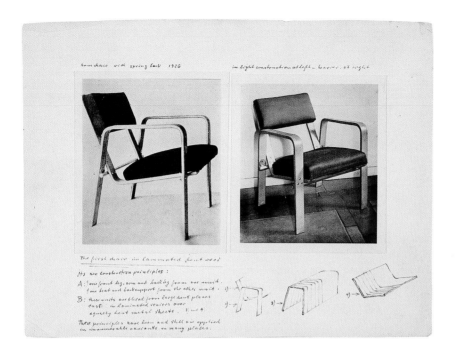

48 JOSEF ALBERS
Photographs and schematic designs of two chairs, n.d.
Two photographs, graphite, and ink on paper
9 ⅜ × 13 ins (24.5 × 28 cm)
Bethany CT, The Josef and Anni Albers Foundation

49 JOSEF ALBERS
*Living room of an apartment for the German Building
Exhibition, Berlin*, 1931
Gelatin silver print
Berlin, Bauhaus-Archiv

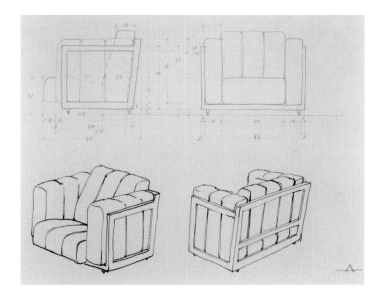

50 JOSEF ALBERS
*Design for an upholstered armchair
for Pauline Schwickert*, 1931
Pencil and india ink on paper
Berlin, Bauhaus-Archiv

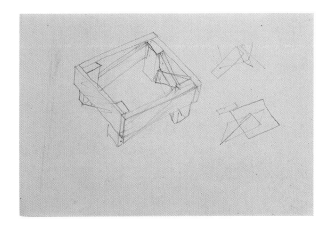

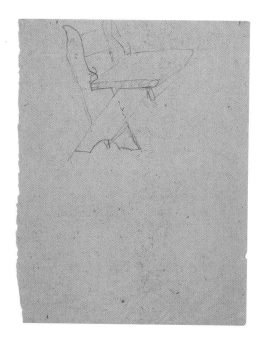

51 JOSEF ALBERS
Study for furniture, n.d.
Pencil on wove paper
4 × 6 ins (10.2 × 15.2 cm)
Bethany CT, The Josef and Anni Albers Foundation

52 JOSEF ALBERS
Study for a chair, n.d.
Pencil on wove paper
5 ½ × 4 ¼ ins (14 × 10.8 cm)
Bethany CT, The Josef and Anni Albers Foundation

(top)
53 JOSEF ALBERS
Bed, *c.* 1927
Walnut veneer and metal
32 × 80 × 40 ins (81.3 × 203.2 × 101.6 cm)
Bethany CT, The Josef and Anni Albers Foundation

(above)
54 JOSEF ALBERS
Pair of night tables, *c.* 1927
Wood and frosted glass
Each 28 ¼ × 14 ¾ × 16 ¾ ins (71.8 × 37.5 × 42.5 cm)
Bethany CT, The Josef and Anni Albers Foundation

(top right)
55 JOSEF ALBERS
Tea table, c. 1928
Ash veneer and milk glass
26 ⅞ × 22 × 21 ¼ ins (68.3 × 55.9 × 54 cm)
Bethany CT, The Josef and Anni Albers Foundation

(above)
56 JOSEF ALBERS
Desk, c. 1940
Wood
28 ⅛ × 83 ¾ × 24 ⅞ ins (71.4 × 212.7 × 63.2 cm)
Bethany CT, The Josef and Anni Albers Foundation

57 JOSEF ALBERS
Study for a table (b), n.d.
Pencil, red pencil, and blue pencil on wove paper
11 × 8 ½ ins (27.9 × 21.6 cm)
Bethany CT, The Josef and Anni Albers Foundation

58 JOSEF ALBERS
Studies for a slung leather chair, c. 1940
Pencil and black ink on wove paper
8 ½ × 11 ins (21.6 × 27.9 cm)
Bethany CT, The Josef and Anni Albers Foundation

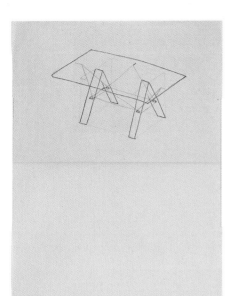

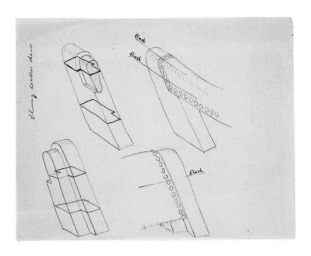

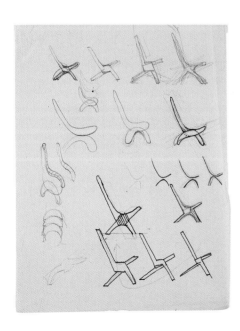

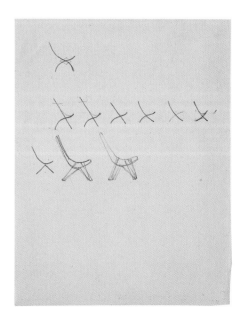

59 JOSEF ALBERS
Studies for Mexican chair, c. 1940
Pencil, red pencil, and black ink on fine
wove paper
11 × 8 ½ ins (27.9 × 21.6 cm)
Bethany CT, The Josef and Anni Albers Foundation

60 JOSEF ALBERS
Study for Mexican chair, c. 1940
Pencil on fine wove paper
11 × 8 ½ ins (27.9 × 21.6 cm)
Bethany CT, The Josef and Anni Albers Foundation

61 JOSEF ALBERS
Study for a desk (a), c. 1940
Pencil on wove paper
5 ½ × 8 ½ ins (13.8 × 21.6 cm)
Bethany CT, The Josef and Anni Albers Foundation

62 JOSEF ALBERS
Study for a shelf, n.d.
Pencil on wove paper
6 × 4 ins (15.2 × 10.2 cm)
Bethany CT, The Josef and Anni Albers Foundation

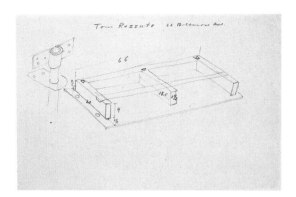

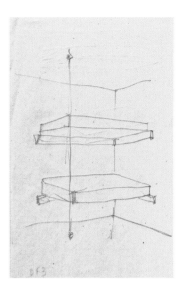

63 JOSEF ALBERS
Architectural studies, n.d.
Pencil on wove paper
4 × 6 ins (10.2 × 15.2 cm)
Bethany CT, The Josef and Anni Albers Foundation

64 JOSEF ALBERS
Studies for an easel, n.d.
Pencil on paper
5 ⅝ × 3 ¾ ins (14.3 × 9.5 cm)
Bethany CT, The Josef and Anni Albers Foundation

65 JOSEF ALBERS
Studies for an easel, n.d.
Pencil and black ink on wove paper
4 ½ × 7 ins (11.4 × 17.8 cm)
Bethany CT, The Josef and Anni Albers Foundation

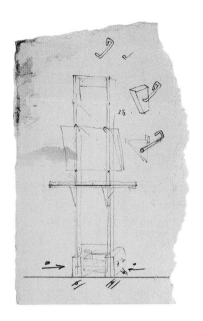

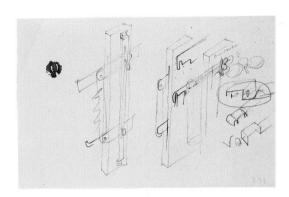

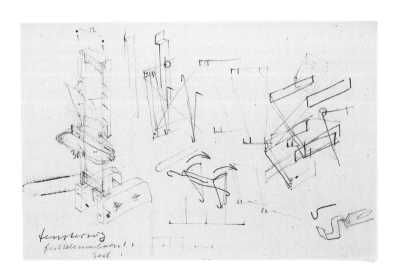

66 JOSEF ALBERS
Studies for an easel, n.d.
Pencil on wove paper
4 ½ × 7 ins (11.4 × 17.8 cm)
Bethany CT, The Josef and Anni Albers Foundation

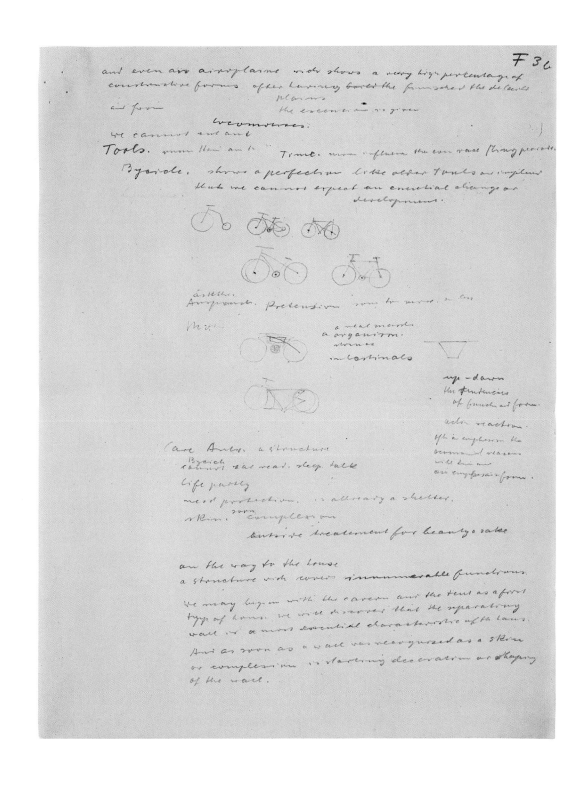

67 JOSEF ALBERS
Hand-written sheet, 'Form and Function', with drawings
of bicycles, n.d.
Graphite on paper
11 × 8 ½ ins (28 × 21.5 cm)
Bethany CT, The Josef and Anni Albers Foundation

(top)
68 JOSEF ALBERS
Fruit bowl, 1923
Silver-plated metal, glass, and wood
2 ⅞ × 14 ⅜ ins (7.5 × 36.5 cm)
Berlin, Bauhaus-Archiv

(above)
69 JOSEF ALBERS
Fruit bowl, 1923
Silver-plated metal, glass, and wood
3 ⅜ × 16 ¾ ins (9.2 × 42.5 cm)
New York, Museum of Modern Art,
Gift of Walter Gropius

(overleaf)
72 JOSEF ALBERS
Study for lettering, c. 1931
Pencil and black ink on orange graph paper
8 ¼ × 11 ¾ ins (21 × 30 cm)
Bethany CT, The Josef and Anni Albers Foundation

(top)
70 JOSEF ALBERS
Tea glass with saucer, c. 1925
Heat-resistant glass, chrome-plated steel, ebony,
and porcelain
Glass: 2 ¼ × 3 ½ ins (5.7 × 9 cm); saucer: 4 ½ ins
(11.5 cm) diameter
Berlin, Bauhaus-Archiv

(above)
71 JOSEF ALBERS
Tea glass with saucer and stirrer, 1925
Heat-resistant glass, chrome-plated steel, ebony,
and porcelain
Glass: 2 × 3 ½ ins (5.1 × 8.9 cm); saucer: 4 ⅛ ins
(10.5 cm) diameter; stirrer: 4 ¼ × ½ ins (10.8 × 1.1 cm)
New York, Museum of Modern Art,
Gift of the designer

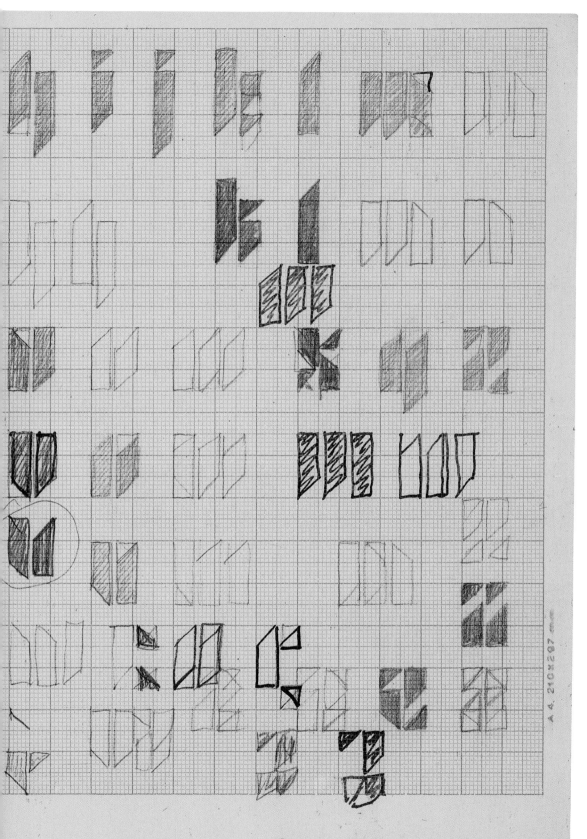

2

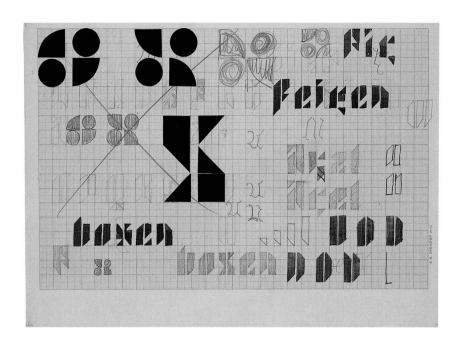

(top)
73 JOSEF ALBERS
Study for lettering, c. 1931
Pencil, black ink, and collage of black paper
on orange graph paper
8 ¼ × 11 ¾ ins (21 × 30 cm)
Bethany CT, The Josef and Anni Albers Foundation

(above)
74 JOSEF ALBERS
Design for a universal typeface, c. 1926
Pencil, red pencil, and black ink on orange
graph paper
8 ¼ × 11 ¾ ins (21 × 30 cm)
Bethany CT, The Josef and Anni Albers Foundation

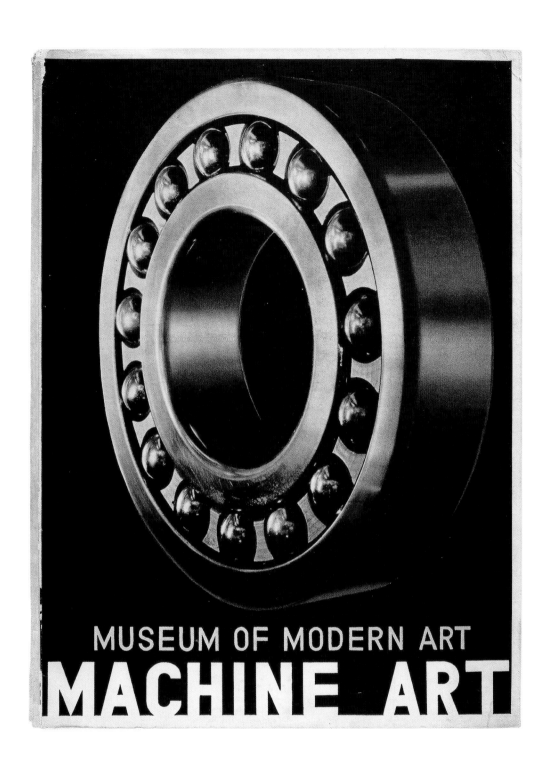

75 JOSEF ALBERS
Catalog cover for the exhibition Machine Art, 1934
Offset printed
9 ¾ × 7 ⅛ ins (24.8 × 18.4 cm)
Bethany CT, The Josef and Anni Albers Foundation

(overleaf)
76 ANNI ALBERS
Sample of leno-weave yard material, 1927
Rayon and synthetic fibers
6 × 4 ⅛ ins (15.1 × 10.5 cm)
Cambridge MA, Busch-Reisinger Museum, Harvard
University Art Museums, Gift of Anni Albers

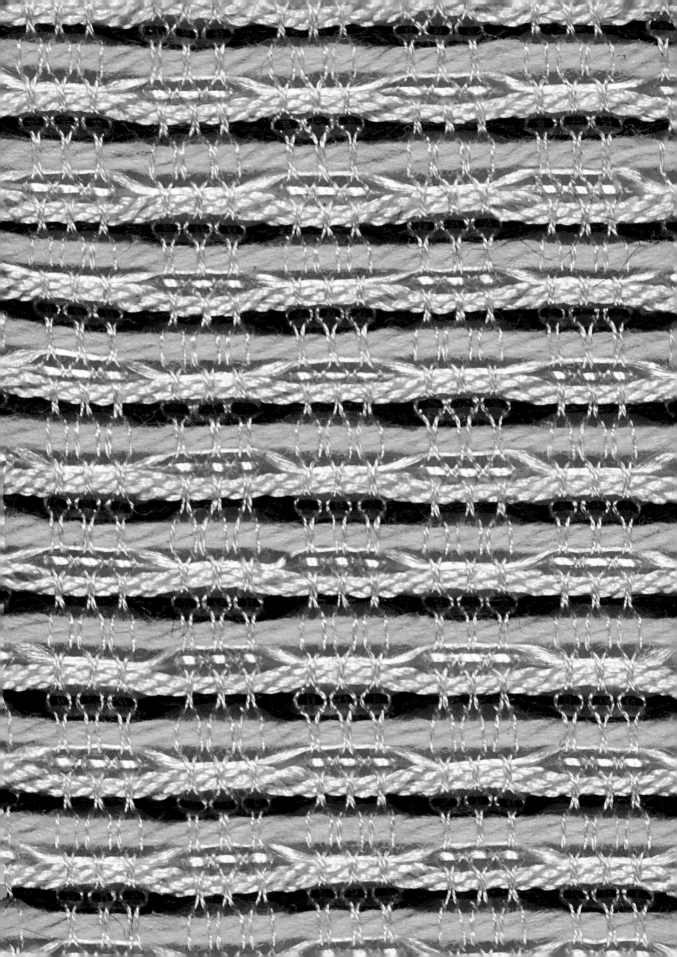

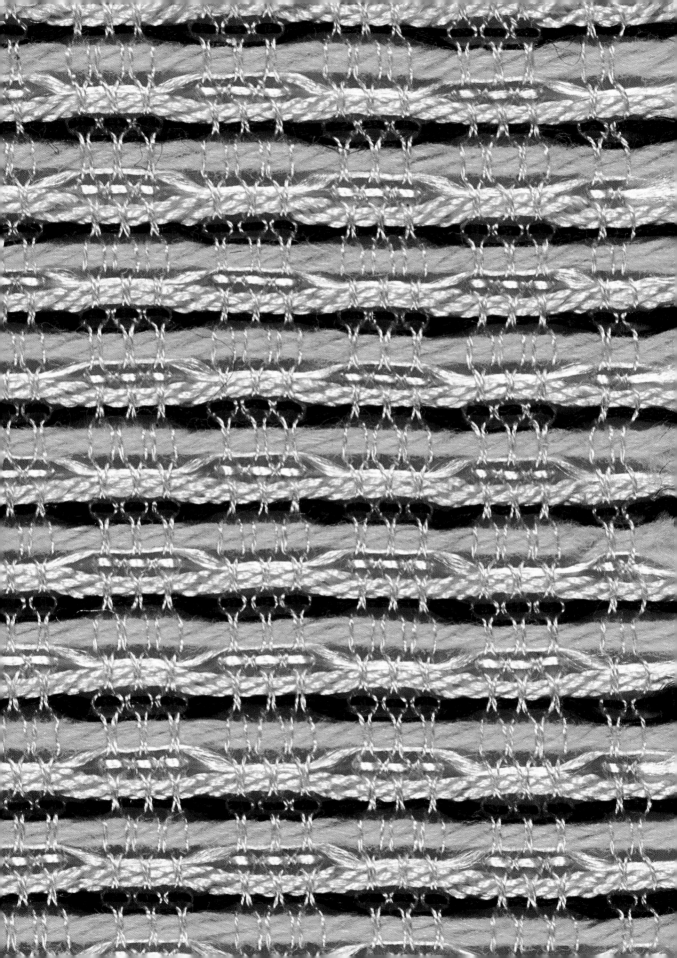

(opposite)
81 ANNI ALBERS
Sample of a wall covering, c. 1928
Jute, twisted paper, and cellophane
6 ¼ × 4 ¾ ins (15.8 × 12 cm)
Cambridge MA, Busch-Reisinger Museum, Harvard
University Art Museums, Gift of Anni Albers

77

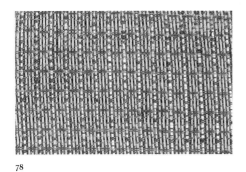

78

79

80

77 ANNI ALBERS
Textile sample, c. 1928
Jute and cellophane
6 × 4 ¼ ins (15.5 × 11 cm)
Cambridge MA, Busch-Reisinger Museum, Harvard
University Art Museums, Gift of Anni Albers

78 ANNI ALBERS
Sample of a wall covering, c. 1928
Jute, twisted paper, and cellophane
6 ¼ × 4 ½ ins (15.9 × 11.5 cm)
Cambridge MA, Busch-Reisinger Museum, Harvard
University Art Museums, Gift of Anni Albers

79 ANNI ALBERS
Sample of bronze and white wall material, n.d
Cellophane and synthetic fibers
6 × 4 ¼ ins (15.3 × 11.1 cm)
Cambridge MA, Busch-Reisinger Museum, Harvard
University Art Museums, Gift of Anni Albers

80 ANNI ALBERS
Sample of black and white wall material, n.d
Cellophane and complex ply linen and
synthetic fibers
6 ¼ × 4 ¼ ins (15.8 × 10.8 cm)
Cambridge MA, Busch-Reisinger Museum, Harvard
University Art Museums, Gift of Anni Albers

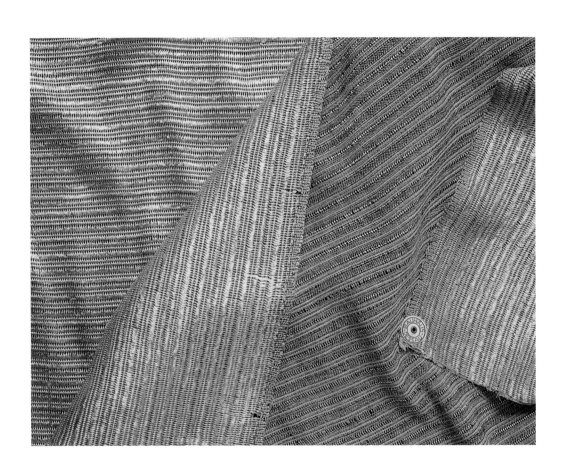

82 ANNI ALBERS
Decorator fabric sample, *c*. 1929
Cotton, rayon, and floss
56 × 78 ins (142.2 × 198.1 cm)
Bethany CT, The Josef and Anni Albers
Foundation, Gift of T. Lux Feininger

83 ANNI ALBERS
Sample of yard material, n.d.
Silk
10 × 8 ins (26.2 × 20.3 cm)
Cambridge MA, Busch-Reisinger Museum, Harvard
University Art Museums, Gift of Anni Albers

84

86

85

87

84 ANNI ALBERS
Drapery material woven for Rena Rosenthal's
*Madison Avenue store, c.*1935
Beige cotton and plastic thread
132 ¼ × 33 ½ ins (336 × 85 cm)
New York, Cooper-Hewitt, National Design Museum,
Smithsonian Institution, Gift of Anni Albers

85 ANNI ALBERS
*Drapery material, c.*1937
Cotton and silk
27 ½ × 21 ins (69.8 × 53.3 cm)
Bethany CT, The Josef and Anni Albers Foundation

86 ANNI ALBERS
*Drapery material, c.*1937
Cotton and silk
30 × 22 ins (76.2 × 55.9 cm)
Bethany CT, The Josef and Anni Albers Foundation

87 ANNI ALBERS
*Drapery material, c.*1940
Linen, rayon, and boucle
93 ½ × 50 ½ ins (237.5 × 128.3 cm)
Bethany CT, The Josef and Anni Albers Foundation

88

89

90

88 ANNI ALBERS
Drapery material for the Rockefeller Guest House, c. 1944
Lurex, cellophane, and cotton chenille
47 ⅝ × 36 ¼ ins (121 × 92 cm)
New York, Cooper-Hewitt, National Design Museum,
Smithsonian Institution, Gift of Anni Albers

89 ANNI ALBERS
Sample for drapery material, c. 1945
Cotton, rayon, and metallic yarn
10 ½ × 7 ⅜ ins (26 × 20 cm)
New York, Cooper-Hewitt, National Design Museum,
Smithsonian Institution, Museum purchase in
memory of Mrs. John Innes Kane

90 ANNI ALBERS
Display fabric sample, 1944
Jute and cellophane
35 × 38 ins (88.9 × 96.5 cm)
New York, Museum of Modern Art,
Gift of the designer

91 ANNI ALBERS
Hand-woven drapery fabric, c. 1945
Cellophane and cotton
6 ¼ × 15 ½ ins (16 × 39.5 cm)
New York, Cooper-Hewitt, National Design Museum,
Smithsonian Institution, Museum purchase in
memory of Mrs. John Innes Kane

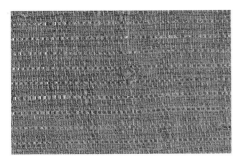

92

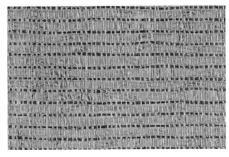

94

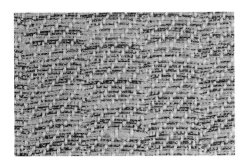

93

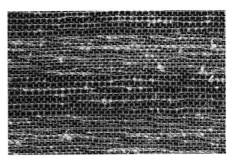

95

92 ANNI ALBERS
Hand-woven sample for a wall covering material, c. 1945
Linen, paper, and cellophane
4 ½ × 8 ¼ ins (11.4 × 21 cm)
New York, Cooper-Hewitt, National Design Museum,
Smithsonian Institution, Museum purchase in
memory of Mrs. John Innes Kane

93 ANNI ALBERS
Hand-woven fragment of evening-coat fabric, 1946
Linen, cotton, and aluminum strips
9 ⅞ × 8 ⅛ ins (25 × 20.5 cm)
New York, Cooper-Hewitt, National Design Museum,
Smithsonian Institution, Museum purchase in
memory of Mrs. John Innes Kane

94 ANNI ALBERS
Hand-woven sample for wall covering material, c. 1945
Linen, cellophane, and paper
4 ¾ × 6 ¼ ins (12 × 15.9 cm)
New York, Cooper-Hewitt, National Design Museum,
Smithsonian Institution, Museum purchase in
memory of Mrs. John Innes Kane

95 ANNI ALBERS
Hand-woven drapery fabric, c. 1947
Cotton
126 ¾ × 46 ⅛ ins (322 × 117 cm)
New York, Cooper-Hewitt, National Design Museum,
Smithsonian Institution, Gift of Anni Albers

96

98

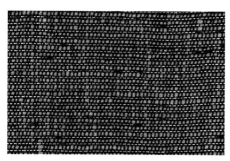

97

99

96 ANNI ALBERS
Hand-woven length designed for a jacket, 1947
Cotton and linen
111 ⅜ × 36 ¼ ins (283 × 92 cm)
New York, Cooper-Hewitt, National Design Museum,
Smithsonian Institution, Gift of Anni Albers

97 ANNI ALBERS
Hand-woven sample for a display material, 1948
Cotton, lurex, and hemp
32 ¼ × 20 ⅛ ins (82 × 51 cm)
New York, Cooper-Hewitt, National Design Museum,
Smithsonian Institution, Gift of Anni Albers

98 ANNI ALBERS
Hand-woven sample, before 1948
Cotton and chenille
7 ⅛ × 11 ins (18 × 28 cm)
New York, Cooper-Hewitt, National Design Museum,
Smithsonian Institution, Museum purchase in
memory of Mrs. John Innes Kane

99 ANNI ALBERS
Hand-woven sample for drapery material, c. 1948
Cotton and aluminum strips
10 ¼ × 7 ⅞ ins (28.5 × 20.4 cm)
New York, Cooper-Hewitt, National Design Museum,
Smithsonian Institution, Museum purchase in
memory of Mrs. John Innes Kane

100 ANNI ALBERS
Free-hanging room divider, c. 1949
Cotton, cellophane,
and braided horsehair
87 × 32 ½ ins (221 × 82.5 cm)
New York, Museum of Modern
Art, Gift of the designer

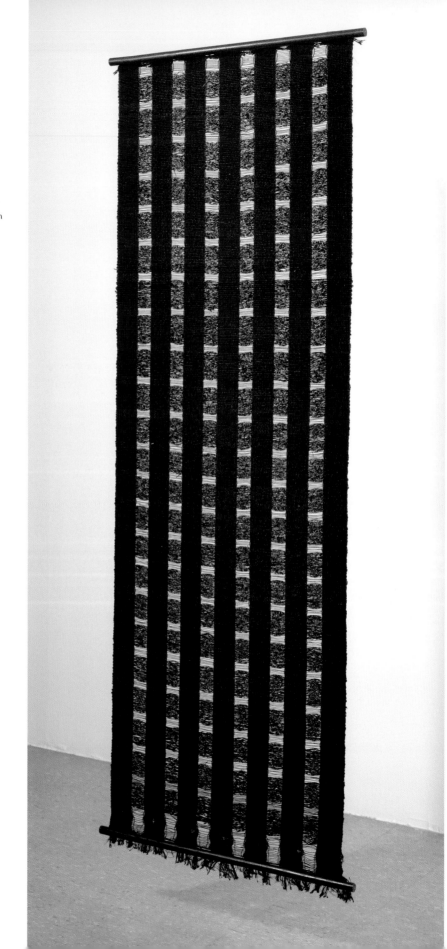

101 ANNI ALBERS
Free-hanging room divider, 1949
Cellophane and cord
94 × 32 ½ ins (238.7 × 82.5 cm)
New York, Museum of Modern
Art, Gift of the designer

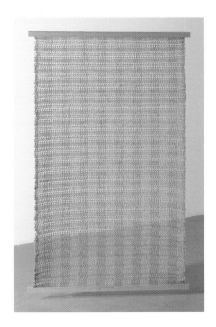

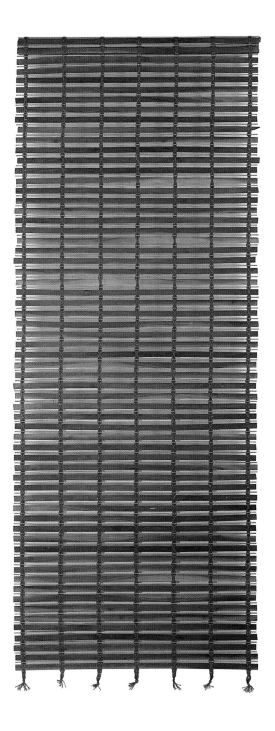

102 ANNI ALBERS
Free-hanging room divider, 1949
Hand-woven jute and lurex
53 × 34 ins (134.6 × 86.3 cm)
New York, Museum of Modern Art,
Gift of the designer

103 ANNI ALBERS
Free-hanging screen, *c.* 1948
Walnut lath, dowels, and waxed-cotton
harness-maker's thread
128 ½ × 42 ½ ins (326.4 × 108 cm)
New York, The Metropolitan Museum of Art

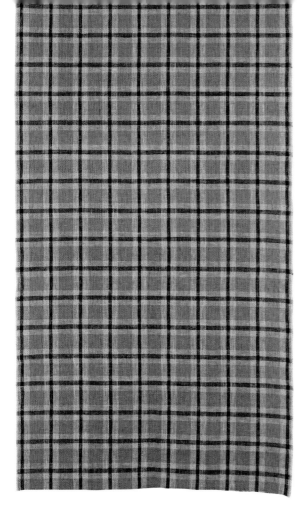

(opposite)

104 ANNI ALBERS
Drapery material for Harvard Graduate Center
lounge, 1949
Cotton and wool
108 ¼ × 50 ¼ ins (275 × 127.5 cm)
Cambridge MA, Busch-Reisinger Museum, Harvard
University Art Museums, Gift of Anni Albers

105 ANNI ALBERS
Bedspread for Harvard Graduate Center
double bedroom, 1949
Cotton
56 × 98 ins (142.4 × 248.9 cm)
Cambridge MA, Busch-Reisinger Museum, Harvard
University Art Museums, Gift of Anni Albers

106 ANNI ALBERS
Bedspread for Harvard Graduate Center
double bedroom, 1949
Cotton
56 × 98 ins (142.4 × 248.9 cm)
Cambridge MA, Busch-Reisinger Museum, Harvard
University Art Museums, Gift of Anni Albers

111 ANNI ALBERS
Hand-woven sample for plain-weave cloth, before 1953
Silk and wool
7 1/8 × 10 5/8 ins (18 × 27 cm)
New York, Cooper-Hewitt, National Design Museum,
Smithsonian Institution, Gift of Anni Albers

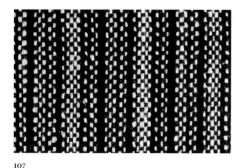

107

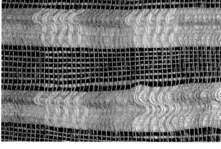

109

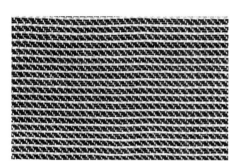

108

110

107 ANNI ALBERS
*Dividing curtain for Harvard Graduate Center
double bedroom*, 1949
Linen and cotton
102 3/4 × 48 3/4 ins (261 × 124)
New York, Cooper-Hewitt, National Design Museum,
Smithsonian Institution, Gift of Anni Albers

108 ANNI ALBERS
*Hand-woven sample with a black-and-white
horizontal stripe*, before 1953
Cotton and rayon
7 1/2 × 10 7/8 ins (19 × 27.5 cm)
New York, Cooper-Hewitt, National Design Museum,
Smithsonian Institution, Gift of Anni Albers

109 ANNI ALBERS
*Hand-woven sample with a subtle horizontal stripe
of black-and-white mixed yarns*, before 1953
Silk and cotton
7 1/2 × 10 7/8 ins (19 × 27.5 cm)
New York, Cooper-Hewitt, National Design Museum,
Smithsonian Institution, Gift of Anni Albers

110 ANNI ALBERS
Open-weave plaid in natural tones, before 1953
Bast fiber, cotton, plastic, and horsehair
12 5/8 × 16 7/8 ins (32 × 43 cm)
New York, Cooper-Hewitt, National Design Museum,
Smithsonian Institution, Gift of Anni Albers

(opposite)
112 ANNI ALBERS
Hand-woven sample, before 1953
Linen
10 ⅝ × 8 ⅛ ins (27 × 20.5 cm)
New York, Cooper-Hewitt, National Design Museum,
Smithsonian Institution, Gift of Anni Albers

113

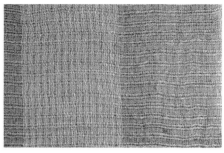

115

114

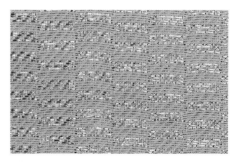

116

113 ANNI ALBERS
Hand-woven sample for drapery material, before 1953
Silk, cotton, and metallic yarn
12 ⅜ × 17 ⅜ ins (32 × 44 cm)
New York, Cooper-Hewitt, National Design Museum,
Smithsonian Institution, Gift of Anni Albers

114 ANNI ALBERS
Hand-woven sample with broad vertical stripes
of tan and off-white, before 1953
Cotton and linen
12 ¾ × 8 ⅞ ins (32.5 × 22.5 cm)
New York, Cooper-Hewitt, National Design Museum,
Smithsonian Institution, Gift of Anni Albers

115 ANNI ALBERS
Hand-woven sample with broad vertical stripes
of off-white and tan, before 1953
Bast fiber
12 ⅜ × 9 ⅜ ins (31.5 × 24.5 cm)
New York, Cooper-Hewitt, National Design Museum,
Smithsonian Institution, Gift of Anni Albers

116 ANNI ALBERS
Woven sample, before 1953
Cotton, paper cord, and aluminum strips
12 ¼ × 17 ⅜ ins (31 × 44 cm)
New York, Cooper-Hewitt, National Design Museum,
Smithsonian Institution, Gift of Anni Albers

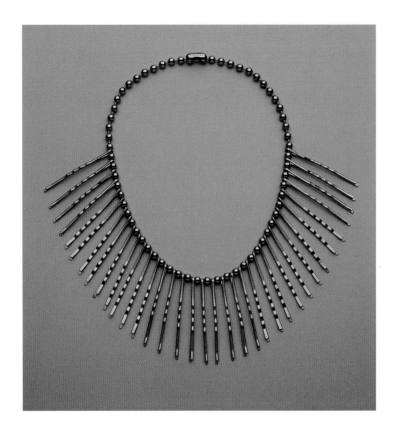

117 ANNI ALBERS
Necklace, c. 1940
Bobby pins on metal-plated chain
Length 15 ¾ ins (40 cm)
Bethany CT, The Josef and Anni Albers Foundation

(opposite)
118 ANNI ALBERS
Necklace, c. 1940
Metal-plated drain strainer, chain, and paper clips
Drain strainer: 3.1 ins (7.9 cm) diameter;
chain: 16 ins (40.7 cm) length
Bethany CT, The Josef and Anni Albers Foundation

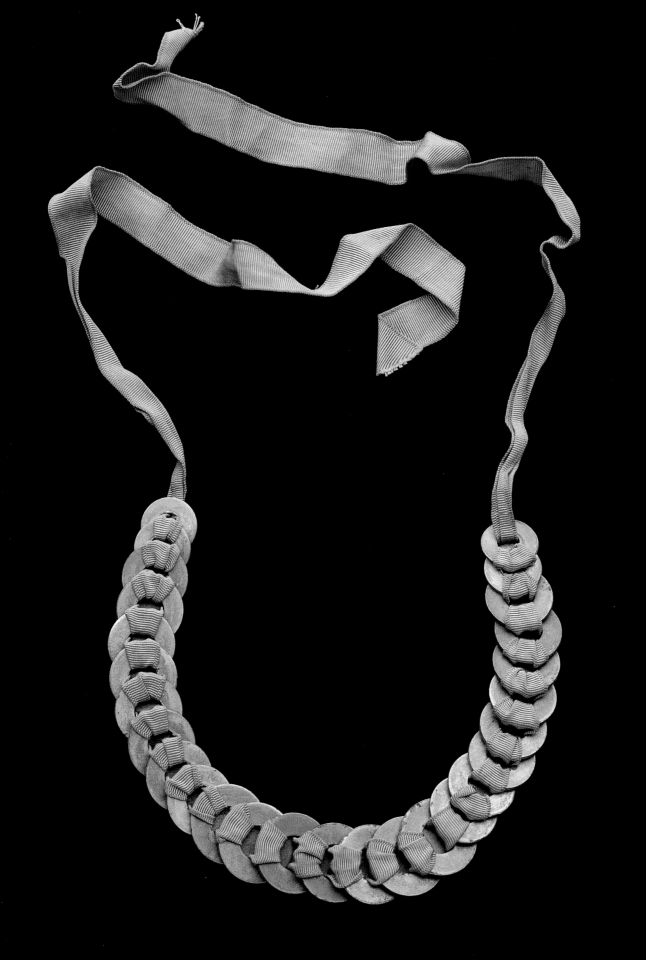

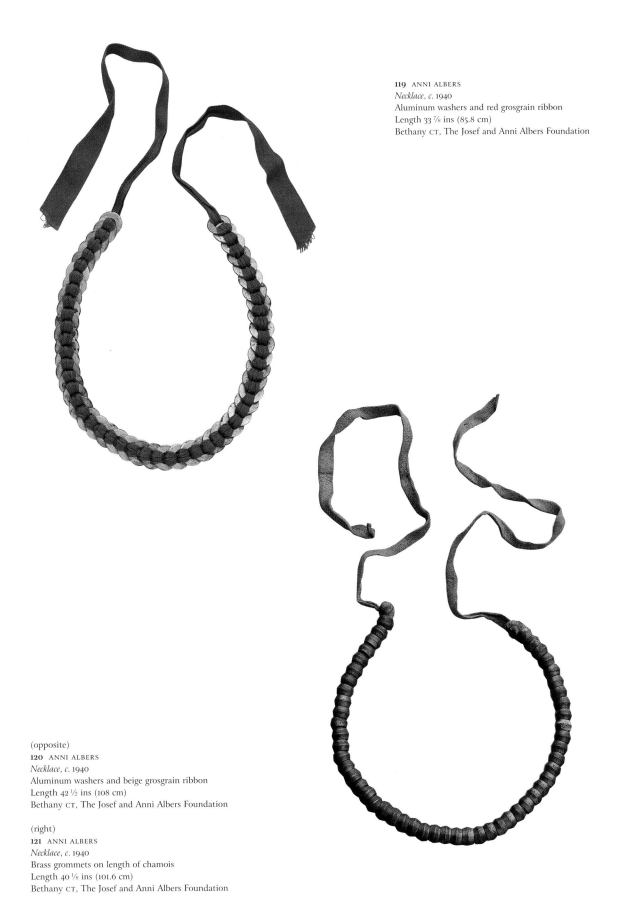

119 ANNI ALBERS
Necklace, c. 1940
Aluminum washers and red grosgrain ribbon
Length 33 ⅞ ins (85.8 cm)
Bethany CT, The Josef and Anni Albers Foundation

(opposite)
120 ANNI ALBERS
Necklace, c. 1940
Aluminum washers and beige grosgrain ribbon
Length 42 ½ ins (108 cm)
Bethany CT, The Josef and Anni Albers Foundation

(right)
121 ANNI ALBERS
Necklace, c. 1940
Brass grommets on length of chamois
Length 40 ⅛ ins (101.6 cm)
Bethany CT, The Josef and Anni Albers Foundation

A MERRY CHRISTMAS AND A HAPPY NEW YEAR A MERRY CHRISTMAS
AND A HAPPY NEW YEAR A MERRY CHRISTMAS AND A HAPPY NEW YEAR
A MERRY CHRISTMAS AND A HAPPY NEW YEAR A MERRY CHRISTMAS
AND A HAPPY NEW YEAR A MERRY CHRISTMAS AND A HAPPY NEW YEAR
A MERRY CHRISTMAS AND A HAPPY NEW YEAR A MERRY CHRISTMAS
AND A HAPPY NEW YEAR A MERRY CHRISTMAS AND A HAPPY NEW YEAR
A MERRY CHRISTMAS AND A HAPPY NEW YEAR A MERRY CHRISTMAS
AND A HAPPY NEW YEAR A MERRY CHRISTMAS AND A HAPPY NEW YEAR
A MERRY CHRISTMAS AND A HAPPY NEW YEAR A MERRY CHRISTMAS
AND A HAPPY NEW YEAR A MERRY CHRISTMAS AND A HAPPY NEW YEAR
A MERRY CHRISTMAS AND A HAPPY NEW YEAR A MERRY CHRISTMAS
AND A HAPPY NEW YEAR A MERRY CHRISTMAS AND A HAPPY NEW YEAR
A MERRY CHRISTMAS AND A HAPPY NEW YEAR A MERRY CHRISTMAS
AND A HAPPY NEW YEAR A MERRY CHRISTMAS AND A HAPPY NEW YEAR
A MERRY CHRISTMAS AND A HAPPY NEW YEAR A MERRY CHRISTMAS
AND A HAPPY NEW YEAR A MERRY CHRISTMAS AND A HAPPY NEW YEAR
A MERRY CHRISTMAS AND A HAPPY NEW YEAR A MERRY CHRISTMAS
AND A HAPPY NEW YEAR A MERRY CHRISTMAS AND A HAPPY NEW YEAR
A MERRY CHRISTMAS AND A HAPPY NEW YEAR A MERRY CHRISTMAS
AND A HAPPY NEW YEAR A MERRY CHRISTMAS AND A HAPPY NEW YEAR
 NEW YEAR A MERRY CHRISTMASA MERRY CHRISTMAS AND A HAPPY

122 JOSEF ALBERS
A Merry Christmas and a Happy New Year, c. 1934
Offset on paper printed in red ink
6 × 9 ins (15.4 × 22.9 cm)
Bethany CT, The Josef and Anni Albers Foundation

123 JOSEF ALBERS
A Good 39, 1938
Postcard with hand-painted alterations
5 ⅜ × 3 ½ ins (13.7 × 8.9 cm)
Bethany CT, The Josef and Anni Albers Foundation

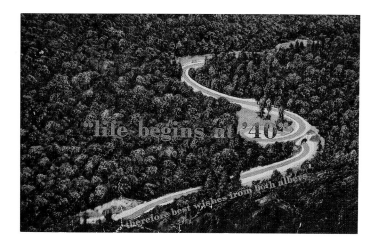

124 JOSEF ALBERS
Life begins at '40/Therefore best wishes from both Albers,
1940
Postcard and transfer lettering
3 ½ × 5 ½ ins (8.9 × 14 cm)
Bethany CT, The Josef and Anni Albers Foundation

125 JOSEF ALBERS
Merry Christmas + Happy New Year, 1941
Postcard with hand-painted alterations
3 ½ × 5 ⅜ ins (8.9 × 13.7 cm)
Bethany CT, The Josef and Anni Albers Foundation

126 JOSEF ALBERS
Merry Christmas + Happy New Year, 1941
Postcard with hand-painted alterations
3 ½ × 5 ⅜ ins (8.9 × 13.7 cm)
Bethany CT, The Josef and Anni Albers Foundation

127 JOSEF ALBERS
With All Best Wishes for '43, 1942
Postcard with hand-painted alterations
3 ½ × 5 ⅜ ins (8.9 × 13.7 cm)
Bethany CT, The Josef and Anni Albers Foundation

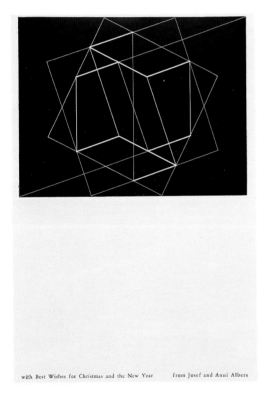

with Best Wishes for Christmas and the New Year   from Josef and Anni Albers

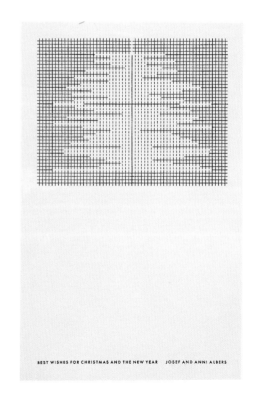

BEST WISHES FOR CHRISTMAS AND THE NEW YEAR   JOSEF AND ANNI ALBERS

128 JOSEF ALBERS
With Best Wishes for Christmas and the New Year/
from Josef and Anni Albers, 1950
Offset on coated paper
8 ⅞ × 6 ⅛ ins (22.5 × 15.6 cm)
Bethany CT, The Josef and Anni Albers Foundation

129 JOSEF ALBERS
Best Wishes for Christmas and the New Year/
Josef and Anni Albers, 1951
Offset on heavy wove paper
8 ½ × 5 ½ ins (21.7 × 13.8 cm)
Bethany CT, The Josef and Anni Albers Foundation

BEST WISHES FOR CHRISTMAS AND THE NEW YEAR   JOSEF AND ANNI ALBERS

130 JOSEF ALBERS
Best Wishes for Christmas and the New Year/
Josef and Anni Albers, 1952
Offset on heavy wove paper
8 ⅜ × 6 ins (21.1 × 15.4 cm)
Bethany CT, The Josef and Anni Albers Foundation

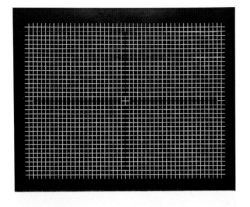

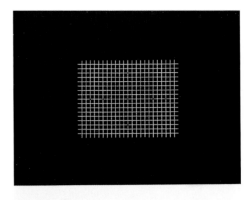

BEST WISHES FOR CHRISTMAS AND THE NEW YEAR   JOSEF AND ANNI ALBERS

BEST WISHES FOR CHRISTMAS AND THE NEW YEAR   JOSEF AND ANNI ALBERS

(above left)
131 JOSEF ALBERS
Best Wishes for Christmas and the New Year/
Josef and Anni Albers, 1953
Offset on coated paper
8 ½ × 5 ¼ ins (21.6 × 13.5 cm)
Bethany CT, The Josef and Anni Albers Foundation

(above right)
132 JOSEF ALBERS
Best Wishes for Christmas and the New Year/
Josef and Anni Albers, 1954
Offset on coated paper
8 ⅛ × 5 ⅜ ins (20.6 × 13.7 cm)
Bethany CT, The Josef and Anni Albers Foundation

(right)
133 JOSEF ALBERS
Happy Christmas and Happy New Year/
Anni and Josef Albers, 1957
Offset on heavy wove paper with deckle edge
4 ¼ × 5 ⅛ ins (10.8 × 13 cm)
Bethany CT, The Josef and Anni Albers Foundation

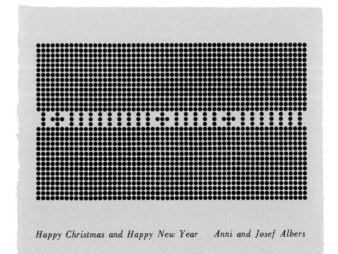

134 JOSEF ALBERS
Happy Christmas Happy New Year/
Anni and Josef Albers, 1960
Offset on heavy wove paper
4 ¼ × 5 ½ ins (10.8 × 14 cm)
Bethany CT, The Josef and Anni Albers Foundation

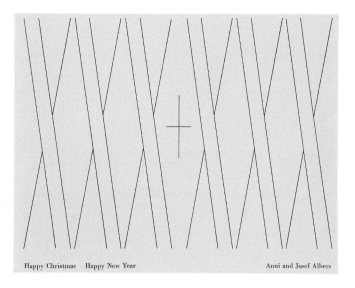

135 JOSEF ALBERS
For Christmas and the New Year from Josef
and Anni Albers, n.d.
Offset on sheet of gray onionskin paper, folded
7 × 12 ½ ins (17.8 × 31.8 cm)
Bethany CT, The Josef and Anni Albers Foundation

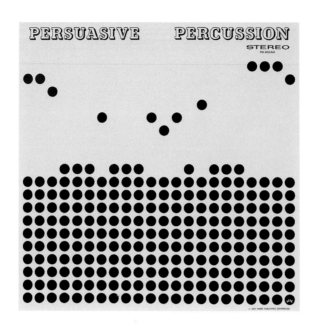

(top)
136 JOSEF ALBERS
Record sleeve: Persuasive Percussion, 1959
Command Records
12 × 12 ins (30.5 × 30.5 cm)
Bethany CT, The Josef and Anni Albers Foundation

(above)
137 JOSEF ALBERS
Record sleeve: Provocative Percussion, 1959
Command Records
12 × 12 ins (30.5 × 30.5 cm)
Bethany CT, The Josef and Anni Albers Foundation

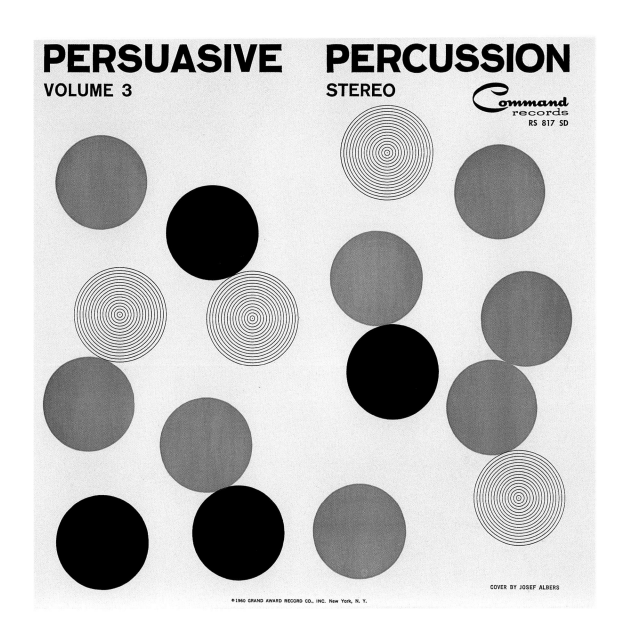

PERSUASIVE PERCUSSION

VOLUME 3

STEREO

Command records
RS 817 SD

COVER BY JOSEF ALBERS

© 1960 GRAND AWARD RECORD CO., INC. New York, N. Y.

138 JOSEF ALBERS
Record sleeve: Persuasive Percussion, Volume 3, 1960
Command Records
12 ⅜ × 12 ⅜ ins (31.4 × 31.4 cm)
Bethany CT, The Josef and Anni Albers Foundation

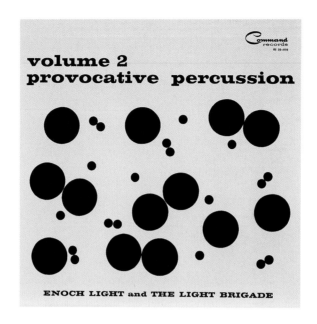

139 JOSEF ALBERS
Record sleeve: Provocative Percussion,
Volume 2, n.d.
Command Records
12 ¼ × 12 ¼ ins (31.1 × 31.1 cm)
Bethany CT, The Josef and Anni Albers Foundation

140 JOSEF ALBERS
Record sleeve: Provocative Percussion,
Volume 3, 1961
Command Records
12 ¼ × 12 ¼ ins (31.1 × 31.1 cm)
Bethany CT, The Josef and Anni Albers Foundation

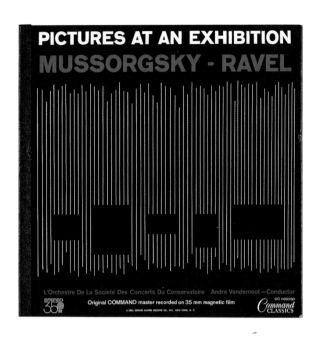

141 JOSEF ALBERS
Record sleeve: Pictures at an Exhibition
(Mussorgsky/Ravel), 1961
Command Classics
12 ¼ × 12 ¼ ins (31.1 × 31.1 cm)
Bethany CT, The Josef and Anni Albers Foundation

142 JOSEF ALBERS
Record sleeve: Leonid Hambro and Jascha Zayde,
Magnificent Two-Piano Performances, 1961
Command Classics
12 ¼ × 12 ¼ ins (31.1 × 31.1 cm)
Bethany CT, The Josef and Anni Albers Foundation

(opposite)
143 JOSEF ALBERS
Maquette for a brick wall (f), c. 1952
Hand-cut wood blocks assembled with glue
6 5/8 × 5 5/8 × 3 1/2 ins (16.8 × 14.3 × 9 cm)
Bethany CT, The Josef and Anni Albers Foundation

144 JOSEF ALBERS
Maquette for a brick wall (e), c. 1952
Hand-cut wood blocks assembled with glue
6 1/8 × 5 1/8 × 1/2 ins (15.6 × 12.9 × 1.1 cm)
Bethany CT, The Josef and Anni Albers Foundation

145 JOSEF ALBERS
Maquette for a brick wall (d), c. 1952
Hand-cut wood blocks assembled with glue
4 3/8 × 5 3/8 × 1 1/2 ins (11.1 × 13.7 × 3.8 cm)
Bethany CT, The Josef and Anni Albers Foundation

(left)
146 JOSEF ALBERS
Maquette for a brick wall (a), c. 1952
Hand-cut wood blocks assembled with glue
7 ³⁄₈ × 7 ³⁄₈ × 1 ½ ins (19.4 × 18.6 × 3.7 cm)
Bethany CT, The Josef and Anni Albers Foundation

(opposite)
147 JOSEF ALBERS
Fireplace, 1955
Off-white firebrick
87 × 64 ins (221 × 162.6 cm)
North Haven CT, Irving Rouse House

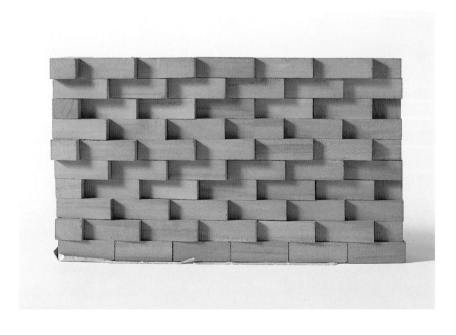

148 JOSEF ALBERS
Maquette for a brick wall (b), c. 1952
Hand-cut wood blocks assembled with glue
5 × 8 ⅞ × 1 ½ ins (12.7 × 22.4 × 3.7 cm)
Bethany CT, The Josef and Anni Albers Foundation

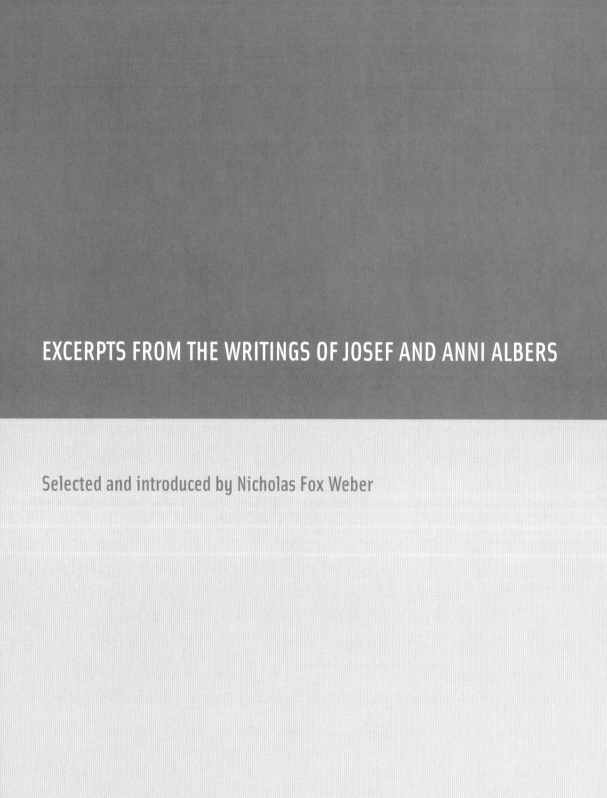

EXCERPTS FROM THE WRITINGS OF JOSEF AND ANNI ALBERS

Selected and introduced by Nicholas Fox Weber

At no time in their lives were Anni and Josef Albers distracted from their focus on everyday aesthetics. They concerned themselves as much with the most minute details—the cost and availability of the right light bulbs, the lining of a raincoat—as with the major philosophical and moral issues embodied by design.

The following excerpts, from letters and essays and unpublished notes, provide a glimpse of their passionate preoccupation with the seeable world.

N.F.W.

From a letter written on Dessau Bauhaus stationery to Josef's friends Franz and Friedel Perdekamp, December 10, 1928:

My dear friends,
Attached are lamp models. They are all very simple and inexpensive. If I knew your rooms, I could recommend something more specific.

For the living room I suggest Me W 94/a. The ball has clear glass in its upper and white glass in its lower part. So semi-indirect lighting. If the rooms have low ceilings, the tube will be shorter …

… Now I wish for you to get your apartment done sooner than I do. Since the holidays we have been living in a Master's House, much too big and too expensive, especially with the crazy heating. Tables only borrowed. Not enough chairs. But empty rooms are really the nicest. Keep your rooms as light as possible and put into them as little as possible, that makes you free …

The Bauhaus lamp prices are for members of the Bauhaus. If required, order through me. Outside more expensive. At Christmas I need to go to the mountains in the snow or I will feel miserable. We have got a three-week holiday—thank God. Now take care and make sure your apartment is clean, light, and empty. Most of your old stuff you don't need any more, and it makes you clumsy.

With best wishes from one house to another,
Juppi and Anni

(Josef's nickname was "Juppi," sometimes shortened to "Jupp.")

Sketch for a light fitting from Josef's letter to Franz and Friedel Perdekamp, December 10, 1928.

Sketch for a light fitting from Josef's letter to Franz and Friedel Perdekamp, December 10, 1928.

From Wohnoekonomie, *written in 1924 by Annelise Fleischmann (who was to become Anni Albers the following year):*

The traditional way of living is an outmoded machine that makes a woman into a slave of the home. Poor arrangement of rooms and furnishings (seat cushions, curtains) take her freedom away and thereby create nervousness and limited possibilities of development.

From a postcard sent on February 9, 1928, to Franz Perdekamp (the Alberses always maintained their fondness for standard units—window panes, hardware, etc.—rather than ones that were difficult to replace):

Dear Franz,
There are already doubts about the flat roof, owing to the fact that our builders are not interested in high-quality work. There are various ways to build the fl. roof. The most important thing is to do it accurately and neatly. Here in Dessau it has worked when it has been done properly. To me the cleverest method seems to be Le Corbusier's, the one he used in Stuttgart. He says using too much reinforced concrete can cause cracks as a result of changes in temperature; over the waterproof roof covering he has a rain-moist layer of sand covered with concrete slabs. Grass grows in the interstices (about 5 cm). He has flowerbeds directly connected to the layer of sand. In this way, the moisture level always stays the same. Builder: Durumfix-Dach Ed Klar u Co GmbH, Stuttgart Ulmer Str. 147.
    Best Wishes,
    Jupp

P.S.: "Experiments" are really unrewarding if the builders are not trained and interested. Thus, this is what I recommend: do not try anything with the walls that is not known there. Also, the flat roof is more expensive, but it provides extra space.—With a house, the inside is the most important thing. Take smooth doors without panes standardized. Smooth doorplates and handles. The Office of Building Construction in Frankfurt used good ones. Walls smooth, sharp edges, no fillet at the thickness. The large space is the best of the room, already all the good Ancients from Egypt to Pompeii and Schinkel knew that, then it got lost. Little, little, little. The empty room is the best!!!!!!!!!!!.

From Anni's 1947 essay "Design: Anonymous and Timeless":

Though only the few penetrate the screen that habits of thought and conduct form in their time, it is good for all of us to pause sometimes, to think, wonder and maybe worry; to ask "where are we now?"

Concerned with form and with the shape of objects surrounding us—that is, with design—we will have to look at the things we have made. With the evidence of our work before us, we cannot escape its verdict. Today it tells us of separateness, of segregation and fragmentation, if I interpret rightly. For here we find two distinct points of departure: the scientific and technological, and the artistic. Too often these approaches arrive at separate results instead of at a single, all-inclusive form that embodies the whole of our needs: the need for the functioning of a thing and the need for an appearance that responds to our sense of form.

This complete form is not the mixture of functional form with decoration, ornament or an extravagant shape; it is the coalition of form answering practical needs and form answering aesthetic needs. Yet wherever we look today we are surrounded by objects which answer one or the other of these demands and only rarely both. If we believe that the visual influences us we must conclude that we are continually adding to disunity instead of to wholeness, that we are passing on the disunity which brought our objects about.

Wholeness is not a Utopian dream. It is something that we once possessed and now seem largely to have lost, or to say it less pessimistically, seem to have lost were it not for our inner sense of direction which still reminds us that something is wrong here because we know of something that is right.

An ancient Greek vase, though unsuited to any use today, still fills us with awe. We accept it as a manifestation of completeness, of true perfection.

A bucket, fulfilling today somewhat the same purpose and functionally far superior to the ancient vessel, embarrasses us and we would blush were our cultural standards to be judged by it. We sense its incompleteness. It is true that some of our technical products today, our chemical glass or china, for instance, or some of the work of engineering, exhibit, in addition to—or by reason of—their clearly defined function, a rare purity of form; they are beautiful. But of the many things that make up our equipment today, hardly any are pure in form though perhaps sufficiently useful. On the other hand, those of our objects which are more concerned with the artistic, the products of our crafts, often are found lacking technologically and are often, if at all, only in part representative of our time.

To restore to the designer the experience of direct experience of a medium, is, I think, the task today. Here is, as I see it, a justification for crafts today. For it means taking, for instance, the working material into the hand, learning by working it of its obedience and its resistance, its potency and its weakness, its charm and dullness. The material itself is full of suggestions for its use if we approach it unaggressively, receptively. It is a source of unending stimulation and advises us in a most unexpected manner.

Design is often regarded as the form imposed on the material by the designer. But if we, as designers, cooperate with the material, treat it democratically, you might say, we will reach a less subjective solution of this problem of form and therefore a more inclusive and permanent one. The less we, as designers, exhibit in our work our personal traits, our likes and dislikes, our peculiarities and idiosyncrasies, in short, our individuality, the more balanced the form we arrive at will be. It is better that the material speaks than that we speak ourselves. The design that shouts "I am a product of Mr. X" is a bad design. As consumers, we are not interested in Mr. X but in his product, which we want to be our servant and not his personal ambassador. Now, if we sit at our desk designing, we cannot avoid exhibiting ourselves for we are excluding the material as our co-worker, as the directive force in our planning.

The good designer is the anonymous designer, so I believe, the one who does not stand in the way of the material; who sends his products on their way to a useful life without an ambitious appearance. A useful object should perform its duty without much ado. The tablecloth that calls "Here I am, look at me," is invading the privacy of the consumer. The curtains that cry "We are beautiful, your attention please," but whisper "though not very practical, we will need much of your time to keep us in shape," are badly designed. The unknown designer or designers of our sheets or of our light bulbs performed their task well. Their products are complete in their unpretentious form.

The more we avoid standing in the way of the material and in the way of tools and machines, the better chance there is that our work will not be dated, will not bear the stamp of too limited a period of time and be old fashioned some day instead of antique. The imprint of a time is unavoidable. It will occur without our purposely fashioning it. And it will outlast fashions only if it embodies lasting, together with transitory, qualities.

(As one may imagine from this text, Anni did not have much time for designers' logos or the flaunting of signatures.)

FURTHER READING

Anni Albers, exhib. cat., essays by Nicholas Fox Weber and Pandora Tabatabai Ashbaghi, New York (Solomon R. Guggenheim Foundation and Harry N. Abrams) 1999

Anni Albers, *On Designing*, New Haven CT (Pellango Press) 1959; 2nd edn, Middletown CT (Wesleyan University Press) 1962

Anni Albers, *On Weaving*, Middletown CT (Wesleyan University Press) 1965; republished New York (Dover Publications) 2003

Bauhaus Furniture: A Legend Reviewed, exhib. cat. by Christian Wolsdorff, Berlin, Bauhaus-Archiv, 2002–03

Neal David Benezra, *The Murals and Sculpture of Josef Albers*, Ph.D. diss., Stanford University, 1983; New York and London (Garland Publishing, Outstanding Dissertations in the Fine Arts) 1985

Black Mountain College: An American Adventure, exhib. cat., ed. Vincent Katz, Madrid, Museo Nacional Centro de Arte Reina Sofia; Cambridge MA and London (MIT Press) 2002

Brenda Danilowitz (ed.), *Anni Albers: Selected Writings on Design*, Middletown CT (Wesleyan University Press) 2000

Mary Emma Harris, *The Arts at Black Mountain College*, Cambridge MA and London (MIT Press) 1987

Josef Albers in Black and White, exhib. cat., essays by J. Stomberg, K.E. Haas, and B. Danilowitz, Boston University Art Gallery; Seattle (University of Washington Press) 2000

Josef Albers Photographien, 1928–1955, exhib. cat., ed. Marianne Stockebrand, Cologne, Kölnischer Kunstverein; Munich (Schirmer/Mosel) 1992

Josef Albers: A Retrospective, exhib. cat., essays by Nicholas Fox Weber, Neal David Benezra, Mary Emma Harris, and Charles Rickart, New York (Solomon R. Guggenheim Foundation and Harry N. Abrams) and Cologne (DuMont Verlag) 1988

Kandinsky-Albers: Une correspondance des années trente, Paris (Musée National d'Art Moderne, Centre Georges Pompidou) 1998

The Photographs of Josef Albers: A Selection from the Josef Albers Foundation, exhib. cat., preface by Nicholas Fox Weber, foreword by John Szarkowski, New York (American Federation of Arts) 1987

Virginia Gardner Troy, *Anni Albers and Ancient American Textiles: From Bauhaus to Black Mountain*, London and Burlington VT (Ashgate) 2002

Sigrid Wortge Weltge, *Bauhaus Textiles: Women Artists and the Weaving Workshop*, London (Thames & Hudson) 1993

Jürgen Wissman, *Josef Albers: Murals in New York*, Stuttgart (Phillip Reclam Verlag) 1971

The Woven and Graphic Art of Anni Albers, exhib. cat., essays by Nicholas Fox Weber, Mary Jane Jacob, and Richard S. Field, Washington, D.C. (Smithsonian Institution Press) 1985

Anni and Josef in the garden of their home at 8 North Forest Circle, New Haven CT, c. 1967.

INDEX

Page numbers in *italic* refer to illustrations.

Aalto, Alvar 45–46, 54
Abstract Expressionism 16
ADGB Bundesschule, Bernau 40
Albers, Anni (née Fleischmann) 9, *14–15*, 17,
    21, *30, 33*, 156, 160
  jewelry (with Alex Reed) 49–50
  textile designs 25–26, 37–43
  WORKS
    Bedspread for Harvard Graduate Center
      double bedroom 127
    Decorator fabric sample 116
    Design for a bedspread 69
    Design for a jacquard weaving 61
    Design for a jute rug 42, 67
    Design for a rug 66
    Design for a rug for a child's room 68
    Design for a silk tapestry 58, 64
    Design for a Smyrna rug 60
    Design for a tablecloth 41, 70, 72
    Design for a tapestry 59
    Display fabric sample 119
    Dividing curtain for Harvard Graduate
      Center double bedroom 43, 127, 128
    Drapery material 118
    Drapery material for Harvard Graduate
      Center 126
    Drapery material for the Rockefeller Guest
      House 119
    Drapery material woven for Rena Rosenthal's
      Madison Avenue store 118
    Drawing for Rug II 71
    Free-hanging room divider 43, 123, 124, 125
    Free-hanging screen 125
    Hand-woven drapery fabric 120
    Hand-woven fragment of evening-coat fabric 121
    Hand-woven length designed for a jacket 122
    Hand-woven sample 122, 180
    Hand-woven sample with a black-and-white
      horizontal stripe 128
    Hand-woven sample with broad vertical
      stripes of off-white and tan 131
    Hand-woven sample with broad vertical
      stripes of tan and off-white 131
    Hand-woven sample for a display material 122
    Hand-woven sample for drapery material
      122, 131
    Hand-woven sample for plain-weave cloth 129
    Hand-woven sample with a subtle horizontal
      stripe of black-and-white mixed yarns 128
    Hand-woven sample for a wall covering
      material 121
    Necklaces 50, 51, 133, 134, 135
    Open-weave plaid in natural tones 128
    Sample of black and white wall material 114
    Sample of bronze and white wall material 114
    Sample for drapery material 119
    Sample of leno-weave yard material 40, 112–13
    Sample of a wall covering 40, 115

    Sample of yard material 117
    Tablecloth fabric sample 70
    Textile sample 114
    Wall hanging 62, 63, 64
    Woven sample 131
  WRITINGS
    "Design: Anonymous and Timeless"
      154–55
    Wohnoekonomie 153
Albers, Josef 9, 13, 21, *30, 33*, 156, 160
  Christmas cards 50–53
  decorative objects 44–45
  furniture designs 10, 11, 24–25, 44–49
  glass designs 10, *11*, 34–37
  graphic design 50–53
  painting 53
  WORKS
    A Good 39 53, 136
    A Merry Christmas and a Happy New Year
      53, 136
    Architectural studies 103
    Armchair 45, 93, 94
    Armchair for Dr. Oeser, Berlin 95
    Armchair, model 97
    Bed 100
    Bedroom stool 88
    Best Wishes for Christmas and the New
      Year/Josef and Anni Albers 138, 139, 140
    Bookshelf/magazine stand 44, 84, 85
    Catalog cover for the exhibition Machine Art
      (1934) 50, 111
    Corner table 92
    Design for an armchair 95, 96
    Design for an upholstered armchair for
      Pauline Schwickert 99
    Design for a universal typeface 50, 52, 110
    Desk 101
    Double armoire 48, 49, 89
    Equal but Unequal 27
    Exhibition display case of oak and glass for
      the 1923 Bauhaus Exhibition 46–49, 83
    Fireplace 53–54, 149
    For Christmas and the New Year from Josef
      and Anni Albers 140
    Fruit bowl 44–45, 106
    Goldrosa 37, 78
    Grid Picture 34–37, 35, 74
    Hand-written sheet, 'Form and Function',
      with drawings of bicycles 105
    Hanging shelf 88
    Happy Christmas and Happy New
      Year/Anni and Josef Albers 140
    Happy Christmas Happy New Year/Anni
      and Josef Albers 141
    Homage to the Square series 18, 20, 25, 34,
      37, 54
    Interior (a) 80
    Interior (b) 81
    Library in Wissinger House, Berlin (with
      Marcel Breuer) 85

    Life begins at '40/Therefore best wishes from
      both Albers 137
    Living room of an apartment for the German
      Building Exhibition, Berlin 46, 47, 98
    Maquette for a brick wall (a) 148
    Maquette for a brick wall (b) 148
    Maquette for a brick wall (d) 147
    Maquette for a brick wall (e) 147
    Maquette for a brick wall (f) 146
    Merry Christmas + Happy New Year 137
    Office desk 87
    Ottoman 46, 90
    Pair of night tables 100
    Park 37, 76
    Photographs and schematic design of two
      chairs 98
    Record sleeve: Leonid Hambro and
      Jascha Zayde, Magnificent Two-Piano
      Performances 145
    Record sleeve: Persuasive Percussion 53, 142, 143
    Record sleeve: Pictures at an Exhibition
      (Mussorgsky/Ravel) 53, 145
    Record sleeve: Provocative Percussion 53, 55,
      142, 144
    Set of four stacking tables 86
    Sideboard 91
    Sketch for a light fitting from Josef's letter
      to Franz and Friedel Perdekamp 152
    Skyscrapers on Transparent Yellow 37–38,
      36, 77
    Sofa in two parts 46, 90
    Structural Constellations 25
    Studies for an easel 104
    Studies for Mexican chair 102
    Studies for a slung leather chair 102
    Study for a chair 99
    Study for a desk (a) 103
    Study for furniture 99
    Study for lettering 108–09, 110
    Study for Mexican chair 102
    Study for a shelf 103
    Study for a table 102
    Table for a reception room 44, 83
    Tea glass with saucer 45, 107
    Tea glass with saucer and stirrer 45, 107
    Tea table 43, 101
    Untitled 34, 75
    Upward 37, 79
    With All Best Wishes for '43 138
    With Best Wishes for Christmas and the
      New Year/from Josef and Anni Albers 138
    Writing desk 87
Amsterdam 50
Amsterdam School 54
Analytic Cubism 37
The Architects' Collaborative 40

Baroni, Daniele 44
Bauhaus 34
  Berlin 11

Dessau 43–45, 50
  Masters' Houses 10, *11*, 24, *24*, 38, 43, 44
  exhibition (1923) 43
  magazine 53
  Vorkurs 34, 38
  Weimar 19, 26, 38–43
Beckmann, Max 18
Berlin 11–12
Berlin, Isaiah, *The Hedgehog and the Fox* 24
Bill, Max 28
Birchwood Drive, Orange, Connecticut *19*
  Anni's bedroom *27*
  Josef's bedroom *29*
  kitchen *17*
  living room *12, 29*
Black Mountain College, North Carolina
  11, 13, 49
  Drs. Fritz and Anna Moellenhoff's living
    room *92*
  Robert E. Lee Hall 13
Breuer, Marcel 24, 25, 43, 44, 45
  Library in Wissinger House, Berlin (with
    Josef Albers) *85*
  Wassily chairs 10, *11*, 46

Calder, Alexander 50
cars 19–20
Cartier-Bresson, Henri 13
Chilehaus, Hamburg 54
Command Records 53
Constructivism, Russian 43
Crystal Palace 45

Dadaism 50
De Stijl 43–44, 53
Dieckmann, Eric 24–25
Doesburg, Theo van 44
Dreier, Ethel 11
Dreier, Ted and Bobbie 13, *16*
dress and appearance 20–24, 30–31
Duchamp, Marcel, readymades 50

Eames, Ray and Charles 34
Eigen Haard housing, Amsterdam 54
Expressionism 18, 34, 37, 43, 50, 54

Feininger, Lyonel 44
Finsterlin, Hermann 39
food preparation and presentation 10, 16, 18
Fuller, Richard Buckminster 25

Gabo, Naum 19–20
Gehry, Frank 39
German Building Exhibition (1931) 46, *47*
Greater Berlin Art Exhibition (1923) 44
Gropius, Walter 10, 40, 43, 45, 53
  Bauhaus Manifesto 38
Guggenheim Museum, Bilbao 39

Harvard Graduate Center 40
Hitler, Adolf 49
Höger, Fritz 54
Horta de Ebro 37
Howe, George, and Lescaze, William 38
Huszár, Vilmos 44

International Style 38, 45, 46
Itten, Johannes 34, 43

Jews 38
Johnson, Philip 11–12, 49–50
Judd, Donald 25

Kairouan, Tunisia 37
Kandinsky, Wassily 25, 26, 34
Karsh, Yousuf 13
Klee, Paul 25, 26, 34, 37, 39, 40
Klerk, Michel de 54
Krajewski, Max 45
Krasner, Lee 34

Le Corbusier (C.E. Jeanneret) 25, 37, 43, 45,
    46, 153
  Ronchamp chapel 25
Lewisohn, Margaret 11
Light, Enoch, and the Light Brigade 53
Litchfield, Connecticut 28
"The Loop" 53

Machine Art (exhibition) 49
Mexico 13, 16, 49
Meyer, Hannes 40
Mies van der Rohe, Ludwig 10, 38, 43, 45, 46
Minimalism 25, 34, 37
Modernism 49, 50
Moellenhoff, Anna 46–49
Moellenhoff, Fritz 25, 46–49
  Drs. Fritz and Anna Moellenhoff's living
    room, Black Mountain College *92*
Moholy-Nagy, László 50
Monte Alban treasure 49
Motherwell, Robert 16–17
Mussorgsky, Modest, *Pictures at an Exhibition* 53

New York
  Cooper-Hewitt Museum 13
  Cosmopolitan Club 11
  Jewish Museum 13
  The Metropolitan Museum of Art 13
  Museum of Modern Art 11, 13, 45, 49
  Sidney Janis Gallery 30
New York Times 16
Newman, Arnold 13
North Forest Circle, New Haven,
    Connecticut *17, 21, 22–23*

Office of Building Construction, Frankfurt 153

Paxton, Sir Joseph 45
Penn, Irving 13
Perdekamp, Franz 152, 153
Perdekamp, Friedel 152
Philadelphia Savings Fund Society 38
Picasso, Pablo 37
Plank House, Orange, Connecticut 16
Pollock, Jackson 16, 34
Preston, Stuart 30

Reed, Alex 49–50
Reich, Lily 10, 11–13
Rietveld, Gerrit 44
Ronchamp, chapel 25

Schinkel, Karl Friedrich 153
Schlumblum, Dr. 16
Sharon-Stölzl, Gunta 39
Snowdon, Lord 13
Stam, Mart 45
Surrealism 50, 53

Thonet (company) 43
Thonet, Michael 45

Warburg, Edward 11, 13, 50
Wilk, Christopher 43
Wingler, Hans M. 39
Worringer, Wilhelm 26
Wu, King-lui *19*, 29, 53–54

Yale School of Architecture 54
Yale University, Department of Design 53

Photographic credits

Anni and Josef, c. 1935.